FISHING THE RIVER OF TIME

TONY TAYLOR

FISHING THE

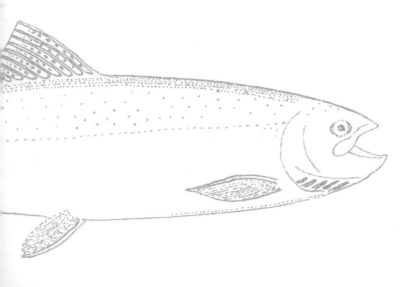

RIVER
OF TIME

GREYSTONE BOOKS

Vancouver / Toronto / Berkeley

Greystone Books Ltd.
www.greystonebooks.com

Cataloguing data available from Library and Archives Canada
ISBN 978-1-77100-057-4 (pbk.)
ISBN 978-1-77100-058-1 (epub)

Cover and text design by W.H. Chong
Cover illustration by Tony Taylor
Map by Kat Chadwick/The Jacky Winter Group
Typeset by J&M Typesetters
Printed and bound in Canada by Friesens
Distributed in the U.S. by Publishers Group West

Greystone Books is committed to reducing the consumption
of old-growth forests in the books it publishes. This book is
one step towards that goal.

To Sara

Contents

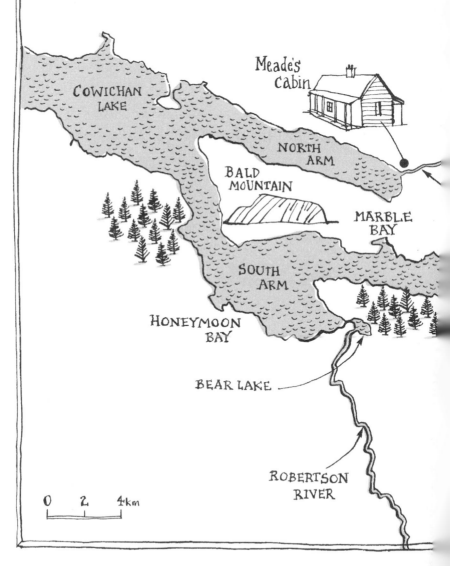

Vancouver Island

Meade's cabin

COWICHAN LAKE

NORTH ARM

BALD MOUNTAIN

MARBLE BAY

SOUTH ARM

HONEYMOON BAY

BEAR LAKE

ROBERTSON RIVER

0   2   4km

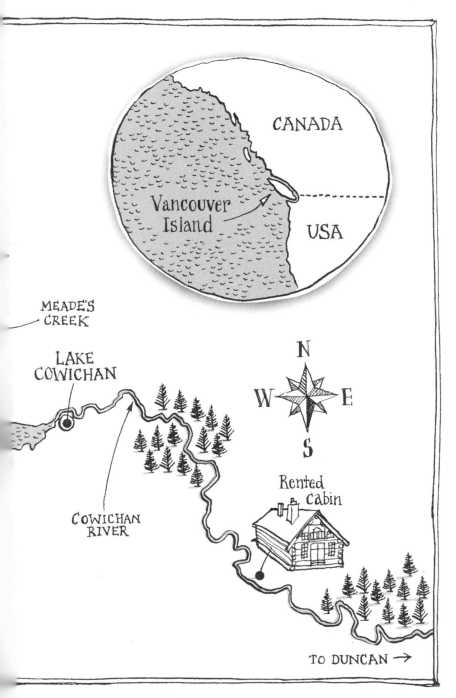

CANADA

Vancouver
Island

USA

MEADE'S
CREEK

LAKE
COWICHAN

N

W   E

S

COWICHAN
RIVER

Rented
cabin

TO DUNCAN →

1

The Fluid World

Life is an adventure searching for answers. They are best looked for in remote places where civilisation hasn't taken hold. High in the mountains, on wild rivers, in the sea. Water, the stuff we are made of, is everywhere; it flows tumultuously, eddies around, twists and turns, slows down, speeds up, then returns to its source. But it can be elusive and mysterious, like truth. Mountains rise to make the rivers, water wears the mountains away, and both give a deeper meaning to time.

Rivers search for the sea and each drop of the magic gets trapped on its journey, moving against the flow at times, before it fulfils its destiny. It is then drawn into the clouds, it rains or snows and the cycle starts over again.

More than any water anywhere else, the water of a young and wild western Canadian river appeared at a critical time in my life, changed a lot of my thinking, and helped show me the way.

Eric Taverner, one of the many fine writers on angling in the twentieth century, used to say to his friends on parting, 'Watch the water.' It was good advice then but it is even better advice today. An angler not only catches fish but also learns a lot by carefully watching water. That is perhaps what angling is really about. The water teaches the watcher about insect life, the way erosion takes place, what the weather is doing somewhere else, how quickly a mountain range is being worn down hundreds of kilometres away and many other things all well worth considering even though it would be tedious to write them all down. That is what we anglers are first: we are water watchers and, because of this but perhaps without realising it, we are prescient about nature and often have a sense of what is going to happen next. We have become guardians of our future simply by sitting by, or walking along, a river. We are not just takers of fish; we are lovers of nature first.

It is May 2008 and, having just separated myself from a slow moving silicate called land, I am travelling through an invisible mixture of gases we call air, crossing the great expanse of another fluid that is the very stuff of life. I am high above the world's largest ocean, flying non-stop for thirteen hours in a twin-engine aircraft from Sydney to Vancouver. The Pacific is so big that if all the land in the world was dropped into it there would still be sea left over. Australia is so far from anywhere its people feel marooned and probably travel more than most. We do it to connect our lives.

I am trying to ignore this contribution to global warming because, if all goes well, in just a few days, I am going to meet my eight-year-old grandson Ned for the first time. I am eighty years old, ten times older than he is, and I figure that if I don't do it now I may not get another chance. I have always been a keen fisherman and I am hoping to teach him to fish.

Fishing, despite its name, I have long understood, is not really about fish. Recently I discovered I was in good company, for about a hundred and fifty years ago Thoreau is supposed to have said, 'Many men go fishing all of their lives without knowing it is not fish they are after.'

Nevertheless it has been good for me to follow rivers, to cast into their depths and occasionally draw out a fish. I have discovered so much more about life and my time on this planet by being footloose with a fishing rod. I hope becoming acquainted with a very special river, quite near his home in British Columbia, will do the same for my grandson.

Ned knows practically nothing about his grandfather except that he lives far away in a place called Australia. Our family has not been good at communicating with one another, but that's a different story. This boy's own adventure I hope will give him something to remember. For it to succeed part of me must go back to being an inhabitant of the bush again, and I have chosen to do it in a place I once knew well.

I rented a log cabin from the Land Conservancy in Victoria, British Columbia's capital city. It was halfway up the Cowichan River and it was remote, but it was more than a cabin, for it had beds for at least a dozen people. But it had no electricity and a pit toilet. The cost was four hundred dollars for the week. I had a set of complicated instructions on how to get there, and despite jet lag and the lack of an adequate map I made it. I was pretty tired after getting off the plane, and driving the small rental car on the wrong side of the road over the fairly long distance to the river right away didn't make a lot of sense. But I was anxious to get to the cabin and settle in.

I left the car, with all its electronic gadgetry, at the end of an old logging road, picked up my swag containing sleeping bag and fishing tackle, and started the walk backwards in time.

I first came to the Cowichan, one of the loveliest rivers anywhere, in 1968 when I was forty. Back then I lived in an abandoned cabin about sixteen kilometres from the cabin I rented now. The wildness of the valley, which was only a few thousand years older than I was and still youthful as natural features go, helped me understand that my years spent working in stodgy museums and university laboratories in England and Australia had been largely a waste of time. Just being in that magical place changed everything for me.

I had worked in the geological section of Britain's wonderful Natural History Museum and had a degree from King's College where, under Charles Lyell, the science of geology had begun. I had taught geology at both Melbourne University and the Australian National University in Canberra and was still passionately interested in the science of the planet, but a prickly feeling under my skin was telling me I had found a modern Garden of Eden; the youthfulness of the river had taken this remote part of the world back to the beginning of time. Here, I thought, I might find some of the secrets of life.

For more than twenty years I had examined the granite cores of mountain ranges in all the great orogenic belts. These deep-seated rocks are known as batholiths and are usually found at the edges of continents where the acid granite pushes up against the more alkaline sub-oceanic basaltic plates. I studied the ancient Caledonian orogeny that, along the line of the Moine Thrust, had finally been torn to bits during the break-up of the world's original continent Pangaea. Parts of these ancient Palaeozoic mountains ended up in Norway, Scotland and Ireland and the rest on the other side of the Atlantic in Greenland, Newfoundland and the Appalachians further south. At the same time I had been studying younger batholiths, more rugged mountains like the Alps and Himalayas. Now I was in part of the world's largest chain forming the rim of the Pacific. This young chain surrounds the world's greatest ocean but the highest parts at the moment are on the eastern side in North and South America. Somehow I knew, deep down inside my bones, the answers were here, where Reginald Daly had discovered the Coast Range Batholith, which stretches from Alaska through British Columbia into Washington State.

Continents are made of granite and there is only enough of this acid rock to cover twenty-nine per cent of our misnamed Earth. They rest on top of an underlying layer of more basic basalt. The remaining seventy-one per cent of this basalt layer is covered with what is actually another more neutral layer, the one that is the source of all life and yet wears all the other rocks down. We call it water.

The highest mountains are usually at the edges of continents where the continual pushing against the hard sub-oceanic basaltic plates causes the granite to thicken upwards as well as downwards forming batholiths, which are the roots of all great mountain chains.

It was not until the sixties that Alfred Wegener's theory of continental drift began to be accepted, although his idea of how the movement came about was incorrect. Nowadays geologists understand the mechanism of plate tectonics and continental drift and can measure the movement very precisely as I did when I went to Greenland in 1957 during the International Geophysical Year. We geologists also understand the importance of the drifting of the different plates of crust in this business of mountain building. The Himalayas and the Alps seem to be exceptions, as there is no ocean near them, but the process is the same: these inland mountains have formed where granite has collided with granite instead of basalt.

I have always been interested in wild places and the connection between rock, water and life; I think of all three as slightly different layers on the surface of our world. It was in estuaries where life originated so the water layer attracted me first. I caught my first fish, with the help of bigger boys, in 1931 when I was three. Fifteen years later I became interested in the fundamental continental material and led a climb up Europe's highest mountain. Mont Blanc is a huge mass of granite. It is very reliable stuff on which to climb. This experience provoked my life-long interest in that rock.

Later, studying the chemistry of mountain roots, I realised the highest peaks occur in the great batholiths where the granite is thickest. Deeply seated granite mountains and stretched granite plains *float* on the underlying basalt that completely surrounds the nickel-and-iron core of the Earth. The mountain ranges as well as the thinner parts of continents float just like blocks of wood do on water with about two-thirds submerged and a third sticking up.

All life forms are based on carbon combined with water, but bacteria, trees, fish and mammals including ourselves, are closely connected to the silicon-based granite, the seemingly infertile mother rock, for life began at the edges of continents in river estuaries. Some species colonised the land and others migrated to the depths of the oceans.

Living in Australia I became interested in Australian rivers and their oxbow lakes, or billabongs, meandering across the dried out silica plains. They were the rivers that had worn the granite away and covered the place with sand. On the west coast of North America I was centrally placed on the Coast Range Batholith where most of the rivers were youthful and straight. I needed to understand why North

America was so rich and fertile while Australia was the Earth's most barren continent.

Quite how I came to live in an abandoned cabin in the Canadian wilderness in 1968 still puzzles me, but it turned out to have been the best thing I ever did. I had recently separated from my first wife and maybe I felt that a sojourn in the deep woods would give me time to sort things out. I had just left a job working for the Countess of Sutherland in the northernmost part of the Scottish mainland. Elizabeth Sutherland, head of clan Sutherland, was desperately trying to right the wrongs of the English duke who had married into this most ancient Scottish family and who had been one of those responsible for the highland clearances in the previous century. She wanted to re-populate the highlands so she moved out of her huge castle, opened the place to the public and set up a school similar to Gordonstoun where Prince Charles was being educated. I was given a magnificent house, called Sportsman's Walk Cottage, and salmon fishing rights on the local rivers. I led mountaineering expeditions and fished with the great Scottish fly fisherman Rob Wilson and the giant Willie Gunn who was faithful servant to Lady Sutherland and in charge of her rivers. I taught Earth science and was also offered the job of curator at the castle's huge wildlife museum which was full of stuffed animals that Elizabeth's childless uncle, the late duke, had shot all over the world. It is one of the world's most beautiful places, but having tasted that kind of freedom I decided I needed to be in an even wilder place.

I knew at once the Cowichan was an exceptional fishery but I had no idea when I first got there it had other claims to fame. Early in the twentieth century the south-ern end of Vancouver Island had been a favourite stopping place for travellers rich enough to circumnavigate the world. I should have guessed because, only a few months earlier, when I was climbing mountains in Assynt examining the remains of the great thrust, I told the Countess of Sutherland where I was going next and she told me Vancouver Island was a lovely place and that I would like it very much. She wished she could have spent more time there. She had been unable to stay long because when she arrived in Victoria Harbour, in September 1939 as a young girl on the duke's yacht, the war broke out in Europe. They had been planning to go bear hunting but the old duke decided to give the huge vessel to the Canadian government as a troop ship. So they took the train across Canada to New York, and travelled home on the *Queen Mary*.

Many British expatriates had returned from India via the Pacific, visiting other parts of the empire, like Australia and Canada, on the way. Many settled in the south-eastern part of beautiful Vancouver Island because the climate was similar to but slightly warmer than chilly England and, more importantly, the cost of living was much lower. Labour was cheap and it was easy to get domestic servants, even if they were more independent in spirit than their British counterparts. Victoria had all the required amenities, and the little town of Duncan, fifty kilometres up the island, was another favourite place to settle. At Duncan they established a lawn tennis club and I was told it had the first grass courts in North America. The British were so successful in establishing an English-style culture that nowadays Canadians refer to Oak Bay on the southern tip of the island being 'behind the tweed curtain'.

I didn't go to Vancouver Island because of the English settlers. If anything the British nature of the place put me off. I was fascinated by the beauty of the area and could not imagine a better combination of mountains and sea. Vancouver Island is a quarter of the size of England but its population was less than that of a small English town. The island was almost all mountains and trees.

The Cowichan River enters the sea at Cowichan Bay, and the town of Duncan is on the river a few kilometres inland. It was in the estuary of this short but powerful river that most of the fishing was done. Salmon would assemble close to the mouth and wait until conditions were just right before running upstream to spawn. At the beginning and the end of these spawning runs the fish are most vulnerable, but in the early days of Europeans on the river few were bothered by that. Not far from the estuary, but still in the bush, was a cabin where the great poet of the Yukon Robert W. Service had lived for a few years as a young man. I don't know if he fished but I am pretty sure he chose to live where he did because he loved to see the great runs of salmon.

I was more interested in the native people than in the English, and I discovered two very different groups. The Cowichan, part of the Coast Salish, lived in the lower country on the eastern shore of the island and they were more involved with the new settlers than those on the mountainous west side. They had a fierce reputation. They hunted grey whales, one of the biggest animals of all, and were knowledgeable about the dangerous tides in the area.

During the next two years I got to know these natives well. I think they appealed to me because they had absorbed little of the culture of the invading Europeans. These brave people were part of what was then called the Nootka (now the Nuu-chah-nulth). In the years that followed Captain James Cook's landing in 1778 they were decimated. There was no war; they died because of European diseases they caught by meeting a few white men. These diseases were unknown to them and included measles, whooping cough, chicken pox, small pox, diphtheria, scarlet fever, tuberculosis and syphilis. Of the 8000 people who had lived at the Nitinat village on the west coast, the Royal Fellowship census of 1863 reported only thirty-five remaining.

About the time of the first world war, a decade or so before I was born, some of the more adventurous European newcomers to the eastern shore of Vancouver Island moved thirty kilometres up the Cowichan Valley. Logging was beginning in the upper part of the valley and a small settlement sprang up at the end of the new logging railway where the river ran out of the huge wilderness lake. Syd Scholey set up a small store and post office at the new settlement and the community came to be called Lake Cowichan.

One of the first to move into that wild country was an old Irish doctor, Dick Stoker, who had retired from the British India army. He was one of four brilliant brothers. They were Bram Stoker who wrote *Dracula* and was also Henry Irving's manager; Sir Thornley Stoker, President of the Royal College of Surgeons; and Thomas Stoker, Chief Secretary of the North West provinces of India. Dick was perhaps the most eccentric of the four. He never returned to Britain, possibly because the fishing in the Cowichan estuary was the best he had ever seen.

Dick Stoker built a house in Duncan and then later a summer bungalow, in an Indian style, on Cowichan Lake. Each year, as one did in India, he moved to higher country in the summer season. He bought the best piece of land at Marble Bay. It stretched right across the Bald Mountain Peninsula, which separates the south arm from the north arm of the lake. It was good land because of a small patch of that rare rock limestone at Marble Bay. The area, like the chalk streams of England, consequently had its own highly specialised insect fauna that attracted large numbers of trout.

The newly married Henry March, an Englishman who arrived at about the same time as Dick Stoker, built the first house in the area, a few kilometres down the lake on the southern shore. He made it out of hemlock logs that nobody wanted and the locals laughed at him for years. This wood was hard to work with and the general view was anyone who used hemlock for anything, except firewood, was a damn fool. People said the house would fall victim to rot, that it was an architectural disaster. But Henry knew what he was doing and had the last laugh, for the house still stands. The community is now called Honeymoon Bay.

Others who arrived later settled where the Cowichan River left the lake, near the small store run by Syd Scholey, but because the trees grew right to the river's edge the rest of the people lived in the twenty or so houses built on log rafts. Scholey's sister married an Englishman named George Simpson. He was knowledgeable about zoology and botany, and was unpopular because he became a kind of self-appointed game warden. The Simpsons were the first to build a float house. When others followed suit, the Simpsons moved down the south arm to Marble Bay from time to time to 'avoid the crowd'. They moored near Doctor Stoker's large log bungalow, for Mrs Simpson and the doctor's wife were good friends.

In 1968 when I went to the lake, the float houses had disappeared and the village of Lake Cowichan had a pub plus a few shops. There were a couple of dozen houses on the side of the river, but the inhabitants still depended on Duncan, thirty kilometres away. To do any extensive shopping one was forced to travel along a very dangerous, narrow and twisty road.

I wanted to live on the water and was lucky enough to be able to rent an old cabin once lived in by a man named Meade. I knew he was a pioneer, but I knew nothing about the literary side of the lake then. Later I gathered this Irishman had a possible connection with the Stokers, but I never discovered what it was.

The cabin suited me; there was a fabulous view down the North Arm. I was surrounded by granite, and every night I watched different sunsets followed by millions of stars that, because there were no other lights, seemed brighter than any I had ever seen. Living simply leads to understanding.

Now, in another century, I was back in this beautiful land living a simpler life once again. The large modern cabin I had rented was a couple of hundred metres away from the river, sensibly built on a piece of high ground. Although I could hear the river, I couldn't see it. The first thing I did was get the fire going and then, ignoring the four bedrooms at the far end, fell asleep on the couch in front of the big iron stove. Sleep I had found impossible on the plane. It had been thirty-six hours since I left my home in the northern suburbs of Sydney. Apart from getting up and throwing another log on the fire once or twice, I didn't wake until well into the next day.

I had plenty of time to prepare for fishing as my grandson would not be delivered to the cabin for a couple of days because of important sporting activities at school: I had chosen an inconvenient time for our trip. Nevertheless, the sun was shining, so after a rather late breakfast I decided to chop more wood before starting to fish.

While I was chopping I wondered what my grandson would be like. I had seen a recent photograph of him and could see a strong resemblance to his father, Matthew, when he was young. It occurred to me then that Matthew must have been about Ned's age when our family had broken up. It was an odd feeling and I felt life was playing a strange game. I had missed out on a great deal of my son's life and now, by going fishing with his son, I felt I was being given a second chance.

Ned had his father's slight build and I think his mother's smile. Looking carefully at the photograph I also thought I could detect a delightful look of mischief in those eyes. I couldn't wait to take him up the river.

2

The Beautiful Simplicity

Fishing is analogous to life and it is best to keep both as simple as possible. The tackle used is always a guide to the angler's character: I use an eleven-foot (3.36-metre) rod with a progressive action. It weighs less than six ounces (156 grams), has a fairly flexible tip and gets stiffer as the strain goes down the rod. Under extreme stress it bends right down into the cork-covered handle at the butt. The curve when a big fish is pulling on the rod is a parabola, identical to the upper quarter of an egg.

Long parabolic rods like this have always been favoured by the highly skilled French market fishermen as well as amateurs like Charles Ritz who, when he returned from America, patented the 'Parabolic' fly-rod and claimed to have invented it. Interestingly these French rods from the home of the metric system are still eleven feet long.

Long before Ritz, in the late nineteenth century, the great F. K. Wallis perfected this type of rod on the Hampshire Avon. It was the first rod light enough to be used with one hand when fishing for trout but long enough and powerful enough to land any salmon. Wallis became famous by using it to cast a small bait weighing only one eighth of an ounce 235 feet (that's three and a half grams, maybe the weight of a worm, cast seventy metres). Allcock's, the fishing tackle manufacturer, later sold copies of the rod as the 'Wallis Wizard', and as far as I know seventy metres is still a record cast. Wallis, however, I am sure, would have been the first to point out long casting has very little to do with actual fishing. He called his rods Avon rods. It's a good name because *avon* is an old word for river.

Rods that bend this way cast well and have recently come into use in America, the original home of the short rod. They are now widely used for steelhead in the American west where they are called 'switch' rods because the angler can use them with either one or two hands.

Fitted to my rod is an old-fashioned free-running 'Aerial' centre-pin reel. It is ten centimetres in diameter and mounted ten centimetres above the butt allowing me to grip the rod's cork handle with two hands if necessary. This centre-pin can be used in two ways for, unlike similar looking 'fly' reels, it can either be allowed to spin freely or prevented from spinning by using the check. Gear like this can cast live bait, worms and lures as well as artificial flies and can be used for any style of fishing in any kind of water. Once mastered, the reel is infinitely superior to either the special fly reels with a built-in drag or the now-ubiquitous complicated and fragile fixed-spool reels. My outfit—the rod, reel and heavy silk line—weighed 450 grams, the same as a cup of coffee.

Fish are remarkably successful creatures having colonised water almost everywhere. Some, such as northern-hemisphere salmon, live and feed in the open ocean but they always return to northern rivers to spawn. Others, like southern-hemisphere bass, live in fresh water but make a reverse journey down river into salt water to spawn. Fish are hard to see which is why sometimes I draw them out just to admire them. Many people fish from curiosity, pulling the beautiful out of the invisible, and only kill when hungry.

Most fish have lots of cartilage around the mouth, which is where the skilful angler hooks his fly. When a fish is properly hooked it feels no pain. It is rather like a human having his or her fingernails trimmed—an inconvenience that we soon get over. Fish are quick learners though, and they soon avoid hooks, so anglers are continually forced to fish remoter places.

So now, forty years after I first saw this river, I am sitting outside a new log cabin preparing to tackle up and I know it will be harder to fish here than it was in the past. But I am back in this beautiful valley not just for the fish. I intend to get to know my grandson and try to help him to love what is wild. And I want to write about all the good things in my life. I hope my grandson will notice that whenever I stop fiddling with my tackle I almost always take out my notebook and write stuff down.

I am here to review every aspect of life and, I have found, I do that best while fishing. For many of us, going into the bush, climbing mountains or canoeing down rivers are ways of coming to terms with reality. To enjoy an outdoor activity it is important to remember it has little to do with reaping a harvest of berries, catching a fish or shooting a deer; it is more about returning to our roots and living simply once again. One thing I am sure of. It is essential for humans to get closer to nature, and, judging from how difficult it was to book this popular cabin, many others think so too.

I am still using the old tapered silk line I bought second-hand from Mick O'Brien the barber at Manuka, in

Canberra, fifty years ago. I think it cost thirty shillings. Now on the veranda of a log cabin far away from Australia, I am threading the green silk through the rings of my beautifully flexible rod. Why barbers nearly always also sold fishing tackle I have never really understood, but perhaps it was to lure us in. I still use these old-fashioned, dual-purpose, tapered silk lines instead of plastic. They handle better, last virtually forever, are heavier, thinner and less affected by the wind than the modern synthetic fly-lines and are therefore easier to cast. Also, because they are thinner they sink better (although not quite as fast as the weighted plastic that contains particles of lead or tungsten), but if you grease them they will float. When greased, even the tip of a silk line floats, whereas the tips of the modern, specially designed, floating plastic lines never do because the thinner tips cannot contain the glass bubbles of air that keep the thicker part of the line afloat.

Ninety per cent of the time trout get most of their food near the bottom and only rise to the surface at the rare times when there is a large insect hatch. So all the angler really needs is a single line that sinks. The silk line has worked for hundreds of years, so why don't anglers use it today? Maybe it's because in the twenty-first century more anglers are fishing very big lakes. The deeper ones tend to develop three layers and the fish are forced to lie in the central zone because the top part of the lake is too hot for them and the deepest part has no dissolved oxygen so the poor things can't breathe. As there is rarely much food in this narrow layer of water the trick is to fish those parts of the lake where the thermocline, as this layer is called, touches the lake's edge. Modern anglers have been brainwashed into buying dozens of 'depth sensitive' lines. The tremendous variety of lines available is a good example of technology getting involved with consumerism and going mad.

When I fish a big lake I wander around the edge until I find a pleasant spot and always use the same slow-sinking silk line.

Perhaps the most important and delightful thing about a silk line is that it can be laid onto the water in a perfect curve with one cast, and the very next cast can be absolutely straight because silk doesn't have the 'memory' problem of plastic. That stuff behaves like a demented bedspring, especially when it is cast from a modern small-diameter reel. As far as I am concerned silk lines have no disadvantages, except perhaps the initial cost (nearly three times as much as plastic lines), but as one doesn't need an assortment of lines, and perhaps spare reels, even that makes sense. Finally, it is better to use silk because it is not a petroleum by-product.

Traditional silk lines are now probably made only in France. They survive there because the discerning citizens eat only wild trout. It is unthinkable for the French to eat pellet-fed fish from biologically unsound fish farms as people do in the rest of the world. Market fishermen fish in the same rivers as ordinary folk and anyone can sell their catch. And these skilful anglers insist on using this thin, sensible line because it catches more fish.

Now the rod is ready to fish I lean it for a moment against the cabin wall. In front of the deck is a small trail going to the left, and fifty metres away a narrow bridge across a gully leads to the water. To the right is another trail and another bridge, over another gully, leading to the end of the logging road where I left my car. Despite the fact it was the smallest, cheapest and most ecologically sensitive transport I could find, I still felt guilty about burning fossil fuel. It added to my guilt about travelling from Sydney to Vancouver Island. I have always been acutely aware of the environmental cost of transport: I was writing about it fifty years ago but so far everyone, including me, has found it easy to ignore.

The bush is fairly thick and hard to push one's way through so it is best to stick to the small trails. Salal and the ubiquitous devil's club are everywhere. This latter plant has huge maple-like leaves and strong stems covered with thousands of barely visible needles that fester beneath the skin if you are foolish enough to try to pull or push the plant out of your way. Also fairly common is the Scotch broom introduced by the early settlers. Fortunately the Atlantic salmon they introduced at the same time did not survive. The biggest trees are maples and most of these are covered in moss. Alder is also common.

The giant cedars and firs that were growing here when the first settlers came to the valley are gone. This part of the river below Skutz Falls was logged the old way by floating timber downstream. All that is left now is second growth; it will take the forest a thousand years to grow back to the way it was. Tiny pentamerous blue and pink flowers grow close to the ground at the edges of the occasional trails. Despite the destruction, seeing nature trying to heal its wounds is rather beautiful.

I am glad I am not burdened with tackle. Anglers are now supposed to need a number of rods instead of one— most wear fully loaded fishing vests and use guides who carry a hell of a lot of extra equipment unheard of years ago. Worst of all, they wear chest waders and wade in on top of the shallow spawning gravels destroying the eggs.

Lone fishermen, like the kind I used to be, are getting rare. Since the movie *A River Runs Through It*, the number of anglers has increased exponentially. Rivers like the Cowichan are riddled with anglers and there are hundreds of professional guides modelled on Brad Pitt. Nowadays many books and most magazines emphasise fish capture by showing, without remorse, pictures of giant fish held at arm's length by successful trophy-hunting anglers. A hundred years ago anglers were obsessed with numbers but today it is size. The truth is neither is important, but fishing is.

So as I sat on the deck of the cabin, looking down a small gully to the right, I thought of many things. I was doing what anglers have done since the beginning of time. It may be called fishing, but a large part of the activity consists of shedding one's daily worries and letting one's thoughts roam free. That is what all land dwellers do when they start to fish—enter another world.

I thought of Dame Juliana Berners, the Abbess of Sopwell Priory, freed for a short time from her religious duties, fishing the River Ver in 1408. This river was near Saint Albans and not far from where I lived as a boy, but I had not heard of her then because I didn't discover her book *The Boke of Saint Albans*, printed in 1486, until I was an adult. I imagined her with her pilgrim's staff that turned into a six-metre rod; the three-metre hollow butt, with the tip stored inside, somehow fixed to the butt piece, dapping her simple artificial fly close to the bank. Being an intelligent woman, well aware of the acuteness of the fish's vision, she would have been standing well back from the water, probably up to six metres away. Anglers did not cast in those days, because the rods were too heavy, and reels and other sophisticated tackle used in China were unknown in the western world. In England, the silk line had not yet come into use, so instead a lighter and weaker horsehair line was just tied to the rod-tip. It had to come from the tail of a stallion so as not to have been weakened by urine. The fly was probably the one she favoured for odd days in May when there was no hatch. It was the one she called the stonefly, with a body of black wool and, in her words, *lappid abowte wyth blacke sylke*.

I thought how, just before I left Australia, I had used the same material tying the few stoneflies that I thought might be needed on my trip. I prefer tying these larger flies because they are easier for me to see. Stoneflies, as their name suggests, are more common on the faster rivers where there are lots of stones. They also need more oxygen, and faster rivers supply that too. These flies can appear in any month of the year and as they are larger than most other flies they offer the trout a better reason to take.

May is usually considered to be the prime time for trout in the northern hemisphere because of the great mayfly hatches described by Frederic Halford in the 1880s. These spectacular events, which cause the fish to ignore all the other flies on the water, mainly occurred on the world's purest limestone, the chalk, and are far less frequent today.

'Matching the hatch', described by early chalk-stream anglers as when the anglers actually tied artificial flies on the river to represent the fragile natural ones of a hatch, is rarely done in the twenty-first century. Nowadays we try to carry a representative collection of artificial flies in a small box.

Less-pure limestone occasionally does have the odd hatch. Angling writers write about them a lot, but it is mostly wishful thinking. As I was fishing the largest mass of granite on the planet, with no limestone in sight, there was no point in using one of the many smaller mayfly imitations sold in most tackle shops, so I tied on one of my thumbnail-sized stoneflies.

Maybe the abbess used larger flies for that reason too. Anyway, I now had a fly almost identical to hers at the end of my line six hundred years later. The Cowichan was a much bigger and wilder river than the Ver; even in Juliana Berners' time her river, being quite near London, would have flowed through cultivated fields with hedgerows and perhaps a few cattle and sheep. There were still bears and cougars here and it was still relatively wild even though parts of it had been logged.

As always happens when one travels from one time zone to another, my biological clock was taking time to adjust. I did not feel like walking a long distance and certainly did not want to fight my way through lots of thick bush. But I picked up my rod and decided to have a cast or two. Anglers often do this sort of not very intense, exploratory fishing and say to one another, 'Let's just wet a line.' I walked towards the river to do just that.

As I got closer, I knew it would be impossible. The roar of the water was so loud it was clear that the river would be unfishable and dangerous. Then I saw the water. Despite the fact I had known the river well forty years ago, I had never seen it flowing with so much force. While the biggest river in Australia was barely flowing at its mouth, this much smaller river in Canada was washing its banks away and carrying trees and large boulders down to the sea. More important, no fish would be able to see the fly because the water was so full of new sediment. It would probably take days to clear.

I remembered I had bought a newspaper in Duncan and the headline had said something about a missing tourist so I went back to the cabin to read it. A couple of days earlier a young man and his rubber raft had apparently disappeared trying to descend the Marie Canyon which was immediately above the section of water I had just been examining. He had been visiting from Mexico and I wondered if he was a member of the large group that had rented my cabin a week earlier. The newspaper said that the police had thoroughly searched the lower section of the river but so far had found no body.

Perhaps it was a good thing that young Ned would not get to the cabin for a couple of days yet; it would give the river a little time to settle, although there was so much water I was fairly sure it would not be possible to fish for about a week. This was a pity because rivers teach the angler so much more than lakes, ponds and canals can.

Maybe the sensible thing to do would be to go into the town of Lake Cowichan and have a look round. It would be interesting to see how it had changed in forty years. I replaced my rod on the deck against the wall and walked out to my car. I followed a couple of logging roads to the north and soon found the new highway. It was so much better than the old narrow twisty road and the trip took only fifteen minutes.

I parked the car at the Riverside Inn and went to look at the water just below. The pool there, right near where the water left the lake, was much smoother than the river further down, and although it was full to the brim and moving fast I could see the salmon. At first I was surprised but a passer-by reminded me that it was the force of the water that made the salmon run. I thought for a moment, then realised he was right. I could not believe I had forgotten so much.

The salmon were what Canadians call spring salmon or tyee ('chief' in the Chinook language) and the Americans in the republic to the south call kings. The correct name for the spring salmon is chinook. Every one of the six different species of Pacific salmon has more than one name and this causes a lot of confusion. Chinook salmon are always the first to run and are the biggest of all salmon, weighing up to forty-five kilograms each. They are usually fished for at the mouths of rivers while the fish are waiting for enough spring melt-water to come down to allow them to go up. I have never enjoyed fishing for them, as although great to see they are not a lot of fun. And I don't like eating them, as they are just too damned big and they taste rather bland. Many people, though, value them for their size. Chefs love them for banquets—they decorate them like wedding cakes—and big fish are now worth thousands of dollars and are usually exported to places like Paris or Tokyo.

What struck me about this run was that it was so small; instead of the river being packed as it was in the past, there were now only about a dozen fish. The local told me that the run, always triggered by the melting snow, was now complete. But he pleased me by saying that fishing in this pool, where the salmon spawned, had been prohibited for twenty years.

I decided not to cross the bridge to explore the town. I would save that pleasure until my grandson arrived. Still somewhat jet-lagged and rather blurred about what day it was, I worked out if today really was Monday he would probably arrive on Wednesday. I don't cross date lines that often so I forgave myself for being rather stupid about the time. After looking downstream for a further view of the salmon gently hovering near the places where they would soon spawn, I looked upriver. The river left the lake about a kilometre upstream and the Riverside Inn was just upstream from the bridge. I started to allow my thoughts to wander and, like geologists do when they look at anything, I went back in time.

3

Going Back in Time

When I first came to the small village of Lake Cowichan forty years ago, all the important business was done at the pub. I was at the peak of my physical prowess and with my climbing ability could have easily got a job as a high-rigger, but I didn't want to cut down trees. The locals couldn't understand this. Most of the men who lived in Lake Cowichan assumed the trees were there, given to them by this benign land, to be cut down. Or the trees were regarded as things that got in the way and had to be removed. The loggers looked at me with mistrust. They were not used to strangers, especially those who could be rivals. Because of their hazardous work these big men banded together and although they came originally from many different nations they regarded people from outside the valley as foreigners. And foreigners were not welcome.

Most of the loggers thought anyone who endured the tortuous road from Duncan was a fool or a tax collector, so they ignored him. If he stayed he was a problem and problems often led to fights. Every Friday night the population gathered at the Riverside Inn but, although I went there a few times, it was not really my style. I was always an outsider; even in my hard mountaineering days, when people wanted to join me, I often preferred to climb alone. I drank alcohol only occasionally and when I visited the inn I felt like a teetotaller in an unknown country. Someone mixed me a drink of God knows what and I downed it to avoid giving offence. The locals then decided I was no threat, and one logger helpfully found me a place to live at the end of a small creek. I was told it was 'out of town' and perhaps they thought it was where I belonged. It was on the lonely North Arm of the giant lake at the mouth of a small westward running stream. The cabin had everything I wanted: running water, a beach and a view. The isolation suited me. I didn't want a social life: I just wanted to look at the granite, fish a little and write things down.

Gradually the local people accepted me and it was then that I learned I was living in the old Meade place and that the nearby stream was called Meade's Creek. Robert Meade was an Irish remittance man and a bit of a legend around the lake even though he had been dead for years. He came to the then unnamed creek a long time ago and lived in the cabin 'like a Salish from Duncan,' the locals told me, and propped up his life with alcohol. It was not of course put quite like that by these hard-drinking loggers, but it was clear from their attitude that, although they also drank heavily, especially on Friday nights, they despised people who could not handle the stuff. They definitely did not consider themselves drunks. Who built the cabin, or when it was built, they did not know. They never mentioned Doctor Stoker, but later, when I learned about him, I realised the cabin could well have been on the same piece of land as the doctor's house and the two men could have had some connection.

I asked other questions about my predecessor, but it was not even known if Meade fished or not. I felt it was almost certain he did. Later on, other sources confirmed that he spent most of his remittance on booze and that he was found dead in his blankets one snowy winter. Apparently no smoke had been seen coming from his cabin for over three weeks so a search party came from Marble Bay, on the South Arm, over the lower part of Bald Mountain and found him frozen stiff. He obviously came from a family with money for two Hardy rods (one for trout and the other for salmon as was the fashion in those days) and a top quality English double-barrelled shotgun were found on pegs on the wall. A half-filled bottle of the best Scotch whisky, that had failed to keep him warm, was sitting on the table next to his bed. The searchers buried him in his orchard. The stone paid for by someone in England is now gone, or more likely never erected, but I have no doubt something of him is still there. No one, even a dissolute remittance man, could live in such a beautiful place without leaving a lot of good behind.

When I came to the lonely cabin, back then, I was overwhelmed. The journey had been a long one. The narrow road twisted through the forest and it was dark because of the size of the trees. I was travelling through forests of some of the largest red cedars left on Earth. Near the lake, there was a wooden bridge over the creek, and a narrow trail led to a small open meadow with fruit trees. A family of raccoons was feeding on the fallen fruit and a black-tailed deer buck bounded away into the forest. The cabin had its back to the orchard and faced the lake. The large door at the front, big enough to drag a boat inside for the winter, had three steps. There was a bit of grass, some drift logs and then the beach. A huge bigleaf maple overhung the cabin and a giant cedar leaned out across the lake. The water was a steely blue, but it was changing colour fast because the sun was starting to go down. I watched the first of many sunsets. They continued to enthral me because no two were ever the same. I could not believe I had been so lucky to find such a beautiful place.

Inside there was a largish living room, a kitchen and a small bedroom at the back. A narrow staircase led to a simple loft. It is so many years now since I first went to live in the old place but I can still smell the cedar, hear the waves and feel the warmth of the afternoon sun. The lake stretched endlessly to the west and, although I had a small wood-and-canvas canoe and constantly explored and fished the lake and the rivers that entered it, I never reached the end. I could have done perhaps, but I remembered that a man's reach should not exceed his grasp, so I always kept something in reserve.

The area was still wilderness; I was just another pioneer, even though old Meade was before me and before him there was possibly some wandering Iroquois trapper. The Iroquois, the most travelled of all the eastern tribes, went everywhere in Canada getting fur for the Hudson's Bay Company. The important thing was that we all came and went without leaving much mark on the land.

My time at Meade's cabin was very different from my time working in Australia. In Australia I walked for many kilometres to find unweathered rock so I could examine the minerals. I was forced to use explosives to get 'fresh' material, but here on this great Canadian batholith unweathered rock was everywhere and the land was so rich. Why, I wanted to know, was the acid granite of this great batholith so fertile whereas the almost identical granite in Australia needed so much help in getting things to grow?

I decided to start my examination of the granite in Canada by climbing the nearest mountain. Between the two arms, at the eastern end of the lake is the peninsula of Bald Mountain. The part of the mountain seen from the village was covered in trees, but the western cliffs were far too steep for trees to grow so, from the west, the mountain rose out of the lake as a bald mass of this acid rock.

I thought I would make my ascent the easy way first. Immediately to the left, or south, of the cabin, a trail crossed the creek and led to Marble Bay. A branch of this trail went to the right and led to the top of the mountain. It turned into a surprisingly good road, although I couldn't imagine why; clearly it hadn't been used for years. After a short time on this wider trail I realised it must have been made during the war, for the mountain summit was an excellent place to view the west.

I was about halfway up when I saw what I thought was a bear coming towards me in the middle of the road. It was not large and it seemed to walk with an exaggerated swagger. It snarled at me, and it was the wickedest snarl I had ever imagined. At that moment I realised two things: it was not going to get off the road for me, and it wasn't a bear. It was a wolverine. The rolling, swaggering, pirate-like gait should have told me that immediately; but it was the first wolverine I had ever seen. I had finally met the dreaded carcajou, or glutton, the scourge of the north, hated by many and so fierce even grizzlies gave it room. I was carrying a small carbine, more as a companion than anything else, so I could have shot it easily. But I didn't need its fine hide with its frost-resisting fur. I already had a good down jacket for winter, so I got off the road. It growled as it passed, gave me the most poisonous look I had ever seen and continued on its way.

Found right the way across the northern hemisphere, these creatures of legend we call wolverines have always been rare and are lonely, bad-tempered animals. They combine the abilities of the skunk and the bear (in fact, skunk-bear is an alternative name) and they always drive all other animals away from their kill. Powerfully built, they have been known to kill moose, bears and cougars, but they seem to be smart enough never to tangle with men. Perhaps this is because we also have been smart enough to never get in the way of their dinner. Wolverine territories cover hundreds of square kilometres. They are great travellers; they follow roughly circular routes that take several weeks. When they kill something as large as a caribou or elk they stay with it until they have eaten every scrap. That is why they are also called gluttons.

At the top of the mountain was a lookout tower, a kind of cabin attached to the top of four tall trees. A series of ladders led to a trapdoor in the floor and from inside the building I could see for miles, the whole length of the lake and beyond it towards the ocean. The steepness of the rock didn't encourage growth and it was easy to see why the locals called it Bald Mountain. It was an honest name.

I spent some time at the top of the tower feeling something like an eagle. For a moment, I had the impression that I was gliding above the Earth and it was a very satisfying feeling. Anthropomorphism is usually not very smart, but to feel like another living being for a moment or two is not a bad idea. I thought back to the wolverine. I didn't know why at the time, but instinctively I had done the right thing by letting it pass. I think I knew to step out of the body of a man for a few seconds. It is good sometimes not to be too human.

I woke the next morning still thinking about the wolverine. Wolverines are fine mountaineers, capable of traversing precipices, and they are probably the only animal that can catch and quickly kill the tough American mountain goats.

These shaggy looking members of the antelope family are related to chamois and are not really goats. They cling to very steep rockfaces with their special sucker-like hooves, and the males fight by sticking their small sharp horns into each other. Accustomed to bleeding puncture wounds, they continue walking and eating after fighting, or even after being shot; they seem to be impossible to kill with bullets. Young goats are good to eat but hunters don't bother them much, because even if a hunter manages to kill a goat he has to be a skilled rock climber in order to retrieve it. Possibly my wolverine had been checking the rockier part of the mountain hoping for goats.

I never heard a native name for Bald Mountain, but I am fairly certain it must have one because it was known to the Nitinat. These intrepid west coast people I met in my later exploring. They, I believe, were the original inhabitants of the whole of this ancient eastward flowing river system. However, they told me they never travelled inland. They said the wild mountainous and forested country to the east was *mesachie*. This word meaning evil came from the Chinook jargon language, a pidgin mix of English and French created more than a century earlier and used by Catholic priests trying to introduce Christianity in the area.

What was clear to me, when I eventually met the Nitinat, was that they still lived in tune with nature. They connected the area to the east with a giant earthquake that had reversed much of the drainage a few hundred years earlier and enabled the Cowichan River to 'capture' the westward flowing water of the lake. Perhaps the earthquake is what they were referring to when they said the east was evil.

The white man's modern maps name a lesser peak to the south as Mesachie. My theory is the newcomers got it mixed up and the Nitinat were too polite to contradict them. This much smaller mountain is beside a small but very deep lake.

The coastal tribes also used the word *skookum* a lot to describe the place; this is the Chinook word used to describe anything that is big and strong. These natives chose to live by the *skookum-chuck* which supplied almost everything they needed. As *chuck* is water *skookum-chuck* means of course the powerful sea. Their view may have changed now, but at the time I knew them it was this: when everything that is needed is either in the sea or on one's doorstep, why bother to go inland?

As for me: I wanted to know why this land was so rich. I knew from my experience in Australia that soils derived from granite were so acidic that very little could actually be grown in them. However, in this new land there was scarcely any room to move in some places. The bush was thick with countless different types of berries all of which seemed to be good to eat. In other places the trees were so big one could walk for hours on the clear forest floor, as there was not enough light for the smaller bushes to grow. The forests were full of game—deer and elk—and many large predators like wolves, lynx, cougars and bears. Most impressive of all, the rivers were full of fish, including six species of salmon and several different kinds of char and trout. It was like Paradise. Why was this land so bountiful when the chemical composition of the granite on the west coast of Canada was virtually the same as the granite in Australia?

Food was everywhere in the great forest and most local people regarded it as everlasting. At the same time logging was booming, and it was clear in many parts of the valley things were beginning to change. It was also obvious that the ongoing destruction of this great natural beauty was unsustainable.

The men who understood the situation best were the fallers—the men who cut the trees. I remember talking to Swanson the giant Swede who cut down the biggest trees of all. He was lifting the back of my truck out of the ditch it had slid into moments before. He told me sometimes he couldn't bear to think about the way he earned his living and I was staggered to see a tear appear in the corner of his eye. But then he shrugged his huge shoulders and said that every time a logger made a mistake and was killed, two more jumped up to take his place. He would have to go on because he had a family to feed.

I had never seen such trees. It was not only the greatest stand of red cedar anywhere, but there were also belts of giant Douglas firs and huge spruce trees just to the west. These different biomes all ran in a north-westerly direction roughly parallel to the west coast. I learned that the biomass on the batholith was the largest on Earth, ten times the mass of the Amazon rainforest. It seemed strange at first but then I remembered from my earlier training that although tropical biomasses have more species evolving—places like the Great Barrier Reef and the Amazon are incredibly rich in numbers of species—they do not have the *mass*. Huge masses of life are commoner in colder places like the Grand Banks in the Atlantic and here on the Coast Range Batholith.

The trees, of course, appeared to form the largest part of the mass. I measured a freshly cut spruce log soon after I arrived. The lower part of the tree was too big to move. It was seven metres in diameter, the size of one end of a singles tennis court or a third of the length of a cricket pitch. Trees like that store more carbon than thousands of modern consumers could release in a lifetime. Douglas firs are equally huge; one of these can provide enough wood to build more than a hundred houses.

The destruction that was happening in this one small valley was feeding a boom in construction in California. This state, with a population twice that of Australia and much greater than that of Canada, was using everything that the northern part of the great batholith could supply. Politicians, of course, thought this was wonderful for the economy of the province but, like all their kind, they were selling our assets without any thought of the future. The Americans were buying the beautiful Canadian trees for the same price as people paid for newsprint elsewhere. The economy seemed insane to me, for I believed having a simple thing like a knife in one's pocket was far more valuable than money.

Perhaps the largest part of the batholith's great biomass came in from the 'salt-chuck', the Pacific Ocean, every year. Flowing off the great batholith are thousands of rivers, so many in fact that the top layer of the ocean in that part of the world is fresh enough to drink. You have to go down twenty metres in some places to find the salt.

Moving into this fresh water in the ocean were countless billions of salmon smelling their way home from places as far away as the sea around Japan. A fish's brain is Y-shaped with the tiny thinking part at the junction of the Y and two huge O-shaped olfactory organs at the end of the two arms which are directly connected to the nostrils. Using this unique smelling apparatus, the salmon does a complex chemical analysis of the free molecules in fresh water and detects the drops that have come from its home river. They then smell their way back to the very pool in which they were born. The fish fertilise and bury their eggs in the same gravel they hatched in, and then they die. The Pacific salmon is the only creature that does this. Biologists consider this method of reproduction much more advanced and efficient than the repeated spawning of its ancestor the steelhead and its cousin the Atlantic salmon.

From the beginning of my sojourn in Meade's cabin I sensed there was some connection between this process and the immensity and the fertility of the great Canadian forests, but it took me a long time, and a lot of fishing, before I began to understand what was going on.

The Nitinat and other original inhabitants of the British Columbia coast, impressed by the size of everything, called it the Great Land. They came from Asia thousands of years earlier and would never have seen so many huge trees, large animals, like the coastal brown bears that stand about two and a half metres tall, and such huge runs of giant fish. When they named it they meant the whole coastal strip of the great batholith, but today the Americans have stolen the name and use it to describe just the part in Alaska.

It was the waters of the Cowichan, more than any of the rivers I had ever fished, or the mountains I had climbed, that helped show me the way. A great forest always does that. It becomes clear to all who enter it that nature knows best. I had landed in another world and I no longer had access to the latest tools of a university laboratory. It was difficult to get any of the measurements I thought of as facts. In wild places it always is like that. No person who lives in the bush for any length of time bothers to measure the amount of carbon locked up in a tree. They either admire it or chop it down. Yet men who work with their hands are not ignorant fools. The two years I spent on the Cowichan in the great forest of the west showed me that the loggers were honest and thoughtful men. The people with power who paid them, and lived far away, were the real villains. They were the men who blurred the truth. Most of the time what loggers said was closer to reality.

My thoughts kept going back to Australia. It had a lot in common with Canada, yet it was a far less fertile country. Could it be just that water is in shorter supply there, or was there something else?

4

The Duty of Memory

I had been standing on the bridge looking at the salmon and the sight of the huge chinook rolling in the water had just taken me back forty years. An unkind person might have said my mind was wandering, but I would counter by saying that I was being thoughtful.

I understood then I had a duty to record what the area was like all those years ago, so I returned to where I had parked the car, bought a few groceries I probably didn't need and another newspaper to check the date—it was Monday— then got in the car and went back to the cabin I had rented. Because I had been thinking about Meade's cabin I had to be careful to drive in the right direction. The paper told me the body of the young Mexican, and the remains of his raft, had been found some way down the river and that the local people were collecting money to send the dead youth back to Mexico. I thought how sad his parents must be, and I realised I would have to do everything in my power to watch over young Ned. I took out my notebook and wrote this down.

At the same time I thought about our duty to the young. Every older person has a responsibility to pass knowledge on but, when doing so, we have to do it in a way that doesn't put the young person off. The best way, I have found, is a twofold approach. First, write down your feelings and the facts, but don't try to deal with them all; they can be mulled over later. Then, be casual about things and try to draw out what is inside a youngster's mind. Don't try to put things in. There is nothing more satisfying to the young than feeling they can contribute too, so ask kids what they think. It is very easy for oldsters to forget we can still learn a lot from the young.

My view is education is the most important thing, but we don't get all of it by going to school. I have never been much of a diplomat, being somewhat clumsy with my social skills, but I have always been patient with young people and this served me well when teaching. To succeed in this difficult job teachers have to engender wonder as well as interest. I hoped that on this beautiful river I could conjure up some of this magic and that I would be able to show my grandson how to fish.

Geologists have always found it easy to wander through time. But I have noticed that near rivers almost everyone forgets about the clock. Our bodies are largely water and I have no doubt that this is why nearly all humans are distracted in this way.

I fell under the spell of water in 1931 when I was three. My mother took her eyes off me for a moment and I ran away. Fascinated by the small colourful fish spawning in the gravel shallows of the Cranberry Brook, I made my way there with unerring accuracy even though it was a long way from my home. Luckily for me there were big boys there, who had carefully removed their boots to get at the fish, so I didn't drown. I remember I waded into the water still wearing my shoes. Eventually the village policeman found me and took me home to my distraught mother.

Because of that first fishing trip I became aware there were two kinds of people: those who wore good stout boots and had to take care of them, like those boys at the Cranberry Brook, and those rich enough to wear fancy shoes. The older boys were very kind. They showed me how to catch tiddlers and gave me a jam jar to keep them in. To my mother's horror and dismay I wanted to be just like those boys.

Now I am older I meditate and reflect upon life quite often. Water helps people think probably because it continually poses questions. When the water watcher is very young he or she wonders where the water comes from and where it goes. Later he or she wonders what is in it, whether it is fit to drink and other simple things. Then, finally, when you get to my age watching water is similar to owning a huge library. It is a source you frequently consult, because if you have fished it for years you know that somewhere along its length it holds pretty well all the answers.

Nowhere is change more apparent than when you go back to a river you knew in the past. From the moment of getting off the plane and renting the car I was aware that even beautiful British Columbia had changed. The traffic on the roads had increased threefold since my last visit and so had the carrion eaters, the turkey vultures. They were everywhere. Whenever one looked into the sky one saw them circling. They are easy to identify as they carry their wings curved upwards with the pinion feathers spread out, and they are superbly efficient in the way they fly. They always glide slowly and never seem to move their wings—one cannot help but admire the way they ride those thermals.

The bald eagle, mainly a fish-eater, was so common

in British Columbia that in the past I had many times seen more than a hundred feeding on a single salmon-spawning run. But on this visit I noticed the eagle was now almost as rare as it was in the United States. It seemed fish were now in short supply across the whole continent. The New World was ageing fast.

Looking into the town pool at the twelve large salmon had brought a lot back: living in Meade's cabin, my adventures on the west coast and lots of other important things. One of my favourite writers, the tramp-poet W. H. Davies, said it perfectly when he wrote:

> When I look into a glass,
> I see a fool:
> But I see a wise man,
> When I look into a pool.

I told my mother something like that when I was three.

In my experience writing and fishing have always been connected. All good writers fished and it didn't matter what country it was. England always had the best of these wonderful people with Juliana Berners starting it all in 1486 with one of the world's first ten printed books leading to Walton's masterwork *The Compleat Angler* that has run into more editions than any other book. Then came hundreds of others who wrote about this noble pursuit; the long list includes people like Virginia Woolf and even Agatha Christie who used to fish the Dart as a welcome change from mystery writing. Dylan Thomas talked about this phenomenon often and said in a talk on the BBC in 1945 the two best writers of prose so far in the twentieth century were Arthur Ransome and George Orwell. He said it was probably because they fished. Eric Blair liked fishing so much he took the name of Orwell, his favourite river, as a surname and in true angler fashion disguised himself as just another George. Ransome also liked the Orwell River, writing at least two books about it. Dylan Thomas was right, and I wonder where one needs to go to find good fishing writers like these two today.

As I drove back to the cabin I realised the details of my fishing trip with my grandson were still pretty vague. His visit to the river had to be fitted in with a number of other important sports activities that I call *games*. I didn't have much sympathy for these demands but I had to go along with them. Fishing was the low man on the totem pole in this arrangement, and I had to wait.

I got back to the cabin and the long wait began. I had no mobile phone but that was part of the plan; it is to escape from technology that we go into the bush. There was no one to talk to so I wrote in my notebook about the missing trees. Matthew had made it clear that he couldn't say when Ned would be free. Their lives were busy. To ease my nervousness about the meeting, I imagined I was trying to get an interview with the Queen. All I could do was stick around near the river and wait for their arrival.

I thought of the lives led by my step-grandchildren in Australia. My wife's daughter was a high-powered executive for one of the huge corporations. Every day she drove all over Sydney; every other week, it seemed, she flew round Australia and south-east Asia. Yet still she managed to work on her computer, speak on her mobile phone, send text messages to all and sundry and drive the kids in one of the family's numerous cars to netball, soccer and volleyball and to the beach. Her husband helped her but there was no doubt she was a world leader in multi-tasking. My wife and I referred to her as Wonder Woman. We understood completely that being a modern parent was a demanding job, yet at the same time we couldn't understand why such multi-tasking was necessary. In our childhoods we organised our own games. There were few private cars, adults were busy earning a living or doing housework, and we wandered around unsupervised. My wife played in Central Park in New York and I explored the English woods and rivers and talked to gypsies and tramps. No one ever kidnapped or murdered us so why, we wondered, did modern kids need such tight parental control? Is the modern world really more dangerous?

Thinking about it in this remote place in the woods where there were cougars and bears, I decided the media was to blame. Almost every night on the TV in Sydney we hear of violence, of people being stabbed or threatened with knives and, according to the news, terrorists threaten us everywhere.

Animals, I have found, are peaceful most of the time, whereas many of my ancestors, and therefore Ned's, were soldiers, going back as far as Waterloo. I have no hesitation in being critical of their deeds, although, as they were all cannon fodder, I do not blame them. But if I had been around when they were, I would have made every attempt to convince them not to listen to others and to think for themselves. My son now has all their medals including the world's first war medal, a huge chunk of silver, given to our ancestor after Waterloo, and I am sure he shows them all to Ned. I can only hope he tells him that fighting is not only bad, it is also stupid. That I think is why I don't like ball games. Many argue they are useful because they get aggression out of the system, but I am inclined to think they are in reality training for war; some of the most aggressive people I have ever met, especially in Australia, have been players of games.

On the other hand, people who occasionally kill something like a deer or a fish tend to be more reverent towards life. Perhaps it is because they are actually responsible for death. For an old man it is a difficult and complex world; one can only imagine what it's like for a kid.

I went to look at the river again and explored more upstream and downstream to try to find some slower-moving water but my search was in vain. Everywhere the water moved with too much force to fish. I thought of the monsters I had seen in the town pool. No wonder they were as big as porpoises and the kings of fish; they had to be to get up the river.

Over the next six months smaller species of salmon would arrive. There were four other kinds of salmon that would come up this particular river before the winter began. I knew, when I booked, that it was not really the best time for the kind of salmon I preferred to catch, but the cabin was fully booked for the rest of the year. I wanted to show my grandson how to catch trout so I imagined the end of May would be a good time for them. That is true in most places in the northern hemisphere, but I had forgotten about the snowmelt in the coastal mountains of British Columbia. Like the young Mexican, I had made a mistake. All was not lost, however, for I could show Ned what a river in flood looked like, and there were other less-wild rivers in the region where we could fish, as well as many small lakes. We might pick up a homely cutthroat or two.

To fish the big lake would be much more difficult, I

knew from living in Meade's cabin all those years ago. There were fish there, but it was difficult to reach them because, like all big-lake fish, they preferred to live in the thermocline, which varied in depth below the surface according to the direction of the wind as well as the time of day. Water below this layer had insufficient oxygen for fish, and water above it was usually too warm. Fishermen with large boats were able to carry the heavy electronic equipment needed to find these fish, but, even if I had access to this kind of gear, I wouldn't use it. When I hunt or fish, I prefer to use my wits and I like my prey to have some chance of getting away.

Many of the modern techniques of catching fish I consider to be environmentally disastrous. I don't go on about it much and if anyone asks me why I don't use more modern gear I usually say it's too expensive for me; I don't tell them that most of the time it doesn't do what the advertiser says it will, and if it does one becomes guilty of overkill. It's like using an elephant gun to shoot rabbits; it's showing off.

I decided to look at the river again and try casting in a slower backwater. I had only been working my fly for a few minutes when a black-tailed deer appeared and I looked away from the water. They are quite small, about the size of a goat, much smaller than the mule deer found in the coastal mountains or the three even larger species found on the mainland, the caribou, the elk and the moose. The little black-tail hadn't seen me and, as the gently moving breeze was at right angles to the river, she couldn't smell me. She was browsing on several different kinds of plants and she reminded me of a human at the self-serve restaurant in University House in Canberra, always a good place for breakfast. She picked delicately at almost everything.

Black-tails seem unafraid of people and when this one's eyes finally focussed on me and she realised I wasn't just another bush she slowly finished chewing her mouthful of leaves and quietly moved away. Because of the extensive logging in British Columbia today there are probably many more of these deer, as they thrive on the small stuff that springs up after the bigger trees are cut down. Deer are not really animals of the deep forest; they prefer the forest's edge. Logging has increased the amount of fringe areas and with them cougars because the deer provide them with more food. Black-tailed deer are now moving into suburbia and the cougars are occasionally following this easy prey right into town. They are so common today the best way to run into either one of these animals is to play golf on one of the ever-increasing number of golf courses. I have never worried about cougars, and I ignored the deer and carried on fishing.

While I had been thinking about the interconnected-ness of these other animals my fly had swung around to my left bank but, even though I had been watching the deer, I knew it had aroused no interest. If I was eventually going to connect with a fish, I would have to concentrate more. I am not a very good fisherman these days; I rarely fix my mind on what the fly is doing because there is so much else to think about and look at.

This backwater, although flowing with a great deal less force than the main river, wasn't a good place for fish. I knew that but, just like Juliana Berners would have done, I put the fly in the water hoping I was wrong. I cast a few times hoping to pick up a stray trout. My river of course was very different from the River Ver. It was much younger and faster and wilder. The good Dame could never in her wildest dreams have imagined a river quite like this one. But she would have told me, if she had been there, that it was quite impossible to fish.

With her advice in hand I decided to move upstream to see if I could find a more suitable place for my young grandson to fish. He would probably arrive at the cabin the day after tomorrow and I needed to work quite a lot of things out. But water is such fascinating stuff, I didn't get round to them.

I was looking for seams in the stream, those lines that separate faster from slower water, but in the main part of the river the water was so fast it all just seemed to boil. I dipped my hand in and the sheer power of the current nearly sucked me into its powerful flow. The water was icy cold. There didn't seem to be any other backwaters where trout might be getting out of the force of the water. I imagined they were all snugged down on the bottom, hidden behind the larger rocks. The rocks would have to be large, I decided, to withstand the force of the water. This part of the river had recently uprooted some large trees and a bunch of these were lying in the water along the bank, quivering visibly as the river hurtled on. The tops were pointing downstream. A little more time or a little more rain I reckoned and they too would be rushing towards the sea.

The first thing I would have to get across to my grandson was not to go too near the water, so how was I going to help him catch a fish? I wanted to do as much as possible on foot but if the river didn't fall rather rapidly I knew we would have to go further afield. We would have to use my rental car and try other places, the slower rivers that drained into the main lake, and if that failed we would have to fish one of the smaller lakes in the valley. I am not keen on fishing lakes, even though some of them are beautiful. I am not sure why that is so but perhaps it is because I have a roving spirit and identify more with wandering rather than the gentler lacustrine existence.

I went further up the river. I always seem to go

upstream rather than down. In some ways it is harder to
fish this way especially when the river is so full and so fast.
But fish always lie facing the current. They have to do that
in order to breathe. The oxygenated water passes in through
the mouth and the deoxygenated water passes out through
the gills. True, fish often hurtle off downstream when they
are hooked or trying to escape another predator like a large
pike or an otter, but powerful escape movements like this
deoxygenate the blood and when the fish needs to get more
oxygen it has to turn back upstream.

I tried to imagine where the fish were hiding in this
turbulent water. I knew exactly where to find the steelhead
because I had devoted most of my fishing time over the last
forty years to the study of this magnificent fish. But it didn't
look like steelhead water today. Even though these fish can
be found in the rivers of the west in any month of the year
and we know where they sometimes feed, they are the most
elusive as well as the most glorious fish of all. If there had
been any steelhead in this river today they would have been
in the slackest water, no further out than a metre from the
bank. So as not to scare them I kept well back.

I started to think about Ecclesiastes. I was not religious and never paid much attention to the Bible as a child,
but rivers tend to make one think back and I do remember
being impressed by the verse that reads: 'All the rivers run

into the sea; yet the sea is not full; unto the place from whence the rivers come, thither they return again.' That bit obviously got to me. I have been thinking about it ever since. The river I was standing by today was flowing so forcibly it was difficult not to imagine the sea filling right up and flooding the land completely. Yet I knew it would not happen.

Weather systems are crucial to the health of our planet and I was helping to screw them up by flying to Canada to show my grandson how to fish. Why, I thought, couldn't he buy fish in a shop like everybody else? Why was I beginning to doubt? I was sabotaging the project from the beginning. A fisherman has to be an optimist; perhaps this is more important than catching fish.

Eventually I reached the canyon. The water moved with such force here I was sure the granite was starting to tremble, and again my mind wandered into regions I didn't necessarily want it to go. I thought of childhood games like rock, paper, scissors and various old Chinese sayings I had come across over the years. What were they called? Were they koans? Wasn't there something in Chinese philosophy about nothing being harder than water? It was a long time since I had read anything by Lao Tzu but I had a feeling as I stood on the trembling rock at the edge of the surge that he must have experienced something similar to this. In the struggle between rock and water there was a riddle that appeared to have no logical solution so I decided that was enough for the day. I climbed off the shuddering rocks and gave up fishing. I realised that although rock was harder than water, according to the Mohs scale of hardness, if you added time to the equation water wore rock away.

Wandering along any river always opens the mind. I hadn't thought about ancient Chinese philosophers for a long time and I knew little about them. But the brain, although very different from a radio or a television, often works like they do and suddenly changes the channel. Somehow or another the Swedish scientist Svante Arrhenius came into my mind. He was the first modern thinker to become aware of the industrial revolution's effect on the atmosphere, in 1896. Somehow he pushed Lao Tzu to the back of my thoughts.

I first became aware of man's power to change a whole planet in 1939 when my new geography teacher G. A. German told us about the work of his friend Guy Stewart Callendar at Cambridge the year before. Callendar predicted that carbon dioxide produced by industry would gradually make the planet too warm to support life. 'Gag', as we called our beloved teacher, whose real mission in life seemed to be to make us all love maps, told us the Earth could eventually become as hot as our sister planet Venus where the temperature at the surface was more than

400 degrees Celsius. We thought about this for an instant, but put the whole thing on the back burner because the immediate threat was a man called Adolph Hitler. The extreme temperature mentioned by my teacher does not seem scientifically likely now, nearly seventy years later, but there is no doubt that the Earth is getting hotter because of the blanket of carbon dioxide.Callendar's prediction on that was correct.

I walked back to the cabin along the old river road. I hoped to find the logging trail where I had left the car. Then it would be just a short walk to the cabin. I could have gone back the way I came but I had had enough of the river for a while. It wasn't paying off in the way I had planned and it would probably not be possible for my grandson to fish. If I was having difficulty getting my fly near to the bottom, where there was only a slim chance of a fish taking it, in conditions like this how could I expect an eight-year-old to have any success? He could depend on luck, but no good fisherman likes to do this.

Walking back along the forest road, perhaps a kilometre away from the river, I spotted a small lake. It looked tempting. But, despite the conditions, I would start Ned casting on the river where he would learn first about the difficulties of fast water, and also perhaps to avoid trees when casting. Then if the river didn't improve in a day or so we would fish the lake.

I got back to the cabin about dusk. I lit the fire and an oil lamp, cooked up a bit of grub and sat down to the table to eat. I propped up a book to read as I was eating. It was the fifth edition of Izaak Walton's *The Compleat Angler*, first published in 1676. This edition contains a new section on fly fishing added by his adopted son, Charles Cotton. Walton mainly fished with natural bait, so for fishermen attempting to fish with an artificial fly this edition is the best.

I gave up trying to read by the light of the lamp. All sorts of memories were flowing; there was a lot I wanted to pass on to my grandson when he arrived. Again I didn't bother to use any of the dozen or so bunks and on my second night in the cabin I slept on the primitive couch in front of the fire.

5
Living in Meade's Cabin

Back in 1968, I enjoyed my stay in Meade's cabin because it gave me a chance to think. The place was incredibly beautiful; to the west everywhere was still wilderness. It was mine, and the land was so rich it begged to be written about. I wasn't sure if my writing could save the area from the chainsaws for, having been trained as a scientist, my writing skills were few and I had no idea of how it could be done. I had written some accounts of mountaineering in the past, encouraged by the poet-mountaineer Michael Roberts, but I was not a practised writer. Only one thing was certain: the best writing in the world could never do this forest justice.

I thought back to the days at the end of the war when I used to eat smoked salmon when visiting the house in Chelsea that belonged to Michael Roberts and Janet Adam Smith. The magnificent mansion was the former home of Lord Nelson's mistress Lady Hamilton and there was a full sized replica of the Elgin Marbles around the upper part of the wall of the huge drawing room. Roberts and his wife used to have the most wonderful literary gatherings there, and people like T. S. Eliot and Dylan Thomas sometimes visited. In fact anybody who was anybody in the literary world used to gather there about once a month, and I met most of the poets and writers of that time. The poet I wanted to meet the most was W. B. Yeats—I didn't know he was dead.

The only reason a callow youth like me got invited was that I was a mountaineer. I climbed in the Alps with Roberts until his death in 1948. The main thing I remember about these parties was that only some of the visitors were mountaineers; most were poets or writers of one kind or another and many of them fished and liked to talk about it.

Every day living in the old cabin brought something new. Clouds over the mountains, sunshine, a bear on the beach, swallows in the spring, rain in the fall and heavy snow in winter. I chopped firewood and milled some lumber. I built a flat-bottomed skiff and a sledge, made an outhouse and built some bookcases to store my books. When I was not busy around the cabin I made expeditions into the woods or paddled my canoe.

Unlike the boat, which I built myself, the canoe, I bought from the Hudson's Bay Company. It was made in New Brunswick of light white cedar, covered with lightweight canvas and painted green. It weighed eighteen kilograms and was built over a proper canoe mould. It travelled across the country covered in sacking and full of straw. Cost, including the rail transport, was sixty dollars, or about three dollars a kilogram. To build a canoe I would have had to have used the heavier western red cedar, made a mould first and covered it with metal to turn and bend the copper nails. I couldn't have done it for the money.

During the next two years I fished the various rivers around the lake and wrote a weekly column in the local newspaper. I called it *Out and About with Tarka*. The column was ostensibly about fishing and hunting, but it also emphasised conservation, which in those days was a dirty word. I chose Tarka as a pen-name because I had loved the book *Tarka the Otter* as a boy. I had no idea when I started writing that Henry Williamson, the author of that wonderful book, was still alive in Devon. I thought about what I was going to write for my column most of the week, then I produced a detailed drawing in Indian ink, and in the last couple of hours or so before the paper went to press, I scribbled off my story. The editor paid me well, but part of the deal was that he kept the drawings.

I started writing when I first went to the lake because I was appalled by the destruction of the great forest that was happening all around me. I wanted to persuade people that there was a better way. We needed to live with nature, not change it. In the end I aroused the wrath of the British Columbia government by criticising the planned dam on the Peace River. The minister in charge used huge amounts of column space criticising my comments. I think I might have suggested the minister was stupid and he accused me of being a coward because I was hiding behind a pen-name. I also failed to persuade most of the locals, although in the end I did succeed in helping get a large area to the west of the lake preserved as what is now known as the Pacific Rim National Park.

One day I was sitting at my typewriter with the door of the cabin open so I could look out at the lake when suddenly a logger appeared in the doorway. I would like to say as it says in the song, I knew he was a logger 'and not just a common bum, for no one but a logger stirs his coffee with his thumb', but it was late afternoon and the coffee pot was empty. He was wearing what all the loggers wore: a heavy, grey wool button-neck vest, stagged wool pants (shortened so as not to catch on the logs) held up by colourful suspenders and caulked boots. He was acutely aware of the spikes in his boots and didn't enter because he knew he would wreck the floor, but he probably would have trodden on my face with them if we had got into a fight.

'Doing a bit of writing?' he asked.

I was cautious as I didn't want anyone to know I was Tarka so I made light of the typewriter saying I was far from familiar with it (which was true) and that I used it mainly for letters (which was not).

'Thought for a minute you might be that guy that writes that rubbish in the paper,' he said, 'but looking at you I can see you're not a proper writer, although a real writer did live in this cabin once.'

I asked him who it was and he told me it was Negley Farson.

'He didn't know what he was talking about either so we ran him out of town,' he said. We talked a little more and then he left. I had been warned.

Negley Farson wrote for the *Daily Mail* in England and was a favourite of my father's. So after the logger had gone I wrote an excited letter to my dad. I couldn't believe it, I was living in a cabin where a man who was his hero had once lived. Dad liked Farson because he wrote sensitively about nature and adventure and he was a conservationist. My father was retired but had been harbourmaster of the port of London during the war. Like me, he wrote in a small way. His stuff was mainly about the history of sail on his beloved Thames and he published short pieces in various nautical magazines. He didn't make much money out of writing; but he once made four guineas for an article on ships in wartime London. That piece, published in London, was republished without his knowledge in the *Calcutta Times*. But when he received that big cheque from the editor, Dad forgave him.

Farson was also a role model for Hemingway who worked under him in Toronto. Somewhere or other I read that Farson was the only one left standing when they drank together. My father wrote back telling me he had heard that Farson had recently died. Apparently he had been living in Devon for years. His nearest neighbour was Henry Williamson and they were very good friends. I was beginning to wonder if some kind of heavenly puppetry had been going on, but in the end I decided life could be much stranger than I could possibly imagine.

The much-travelled Farson came to Cowichan Lake twice and wrote two books about it. The first time was on his honeymoon in the early twenties—he married Dick Stoker's niece, Eve. That visit produced a depressing novel published in 1938 and called *The Story of a Lake*. It was this book that antagonised the locals. He described them all in so much detail they were easy to recognise and he hardly bothered to change most of the names. It is the story of a drunk living alone in a cabin, like Meade. Yet during the winter Farson and his wife probably stayed in the log bungalow at Marble Bay when Doctor Stoker stayed in Duncan. Always playful with names, Farson called his wife's uncle Feathers because the old doctor was always tying new fishing flies. Eve Stoker, it was said, loved the wildness even more than her husband did, but quite what happened to her and their marriage I have been unable to find out.

Farson returned to the lake, I think alone, and wrote what has been described as one of the greatest books on fishing ever written. *Going Fishing* was published in October 1942 and is kept by most anglers on their shelves next to Izaak Walton.

For the last year or two a British angling magazine has been encouraging its readers to write in every month to list and comment on their six favourite fishing books. Farson and a follower of his, Hugh Falkus, now both long dead, are still two of the most popular authors. Falkus read *Going Fishing* in 1943 when he was a prisoner of war in Germany. How the book got there he does not explain but I imagine some sympathetic person put it in one of the comfort-parcels that were sent from neutral countries to British prisoners of war. If I remember correctly only things like warm clothing and socks were allowed. I like to think that the German guard who inspected the parcel was an angler too and passed it on to Falkus to get some help with translating the English text. Perhaps talking about fishing made them good friends and they went fishing together when the war was over.

Although he considered himself an Englishman, and had been a pilot in Britain's air force during the first world war, James Scott Negley Farson was born in Plainfield, New Jersey, in 1890. His unmarried mother died in childbirth, and the orphan was adopted and raised by an eccentric American Civil War veteran known as 'General'. His name was James Negley and he had no family of his own so he added Negley to Farson's name, apparently to make him his heir, and Farson called the old man Grandfather. Unfortunately for Farson, when the old man died, the big house was repossessed because there was no money to cover his debts.

Reading between the lines of *The Story of a Lake*, it seems to me that Farson poured much of himself plus plenty of whisky into the chief character in the book, and that may have been another reason for its failure. He did, however, become perhaps one of the world's most popular travel writers in the years before the second world war. Although he wrote at least half a dozen successful travel books, sadly, except for *Going Fishing*, all have been forgotten.

Because of my writing about the Peace River

Dam—the disastrous new plan to flood the Rocky Mountain Trench for a hydro-electric scheme—I met Raymond Patterson. His book *The Dangerous River* first appeared in England and Canada in 1954 and has been reprinted two or three times and translated into Spanish, Dutch and other languages. I found the book fascinating because it was about the northern part of the Coast Range Batholith and in it Patterson described his adventures in the great canyon of the Nahanni River. This little-known river with its narrow gorge more than a thousand metres deep is more spectacular than the Grand Canyon, and the huge falls halfway up are similar to those on the Niagara River. Patterson travelled up this river in a wood–canvas prospector's canoe like mine, and we found we had a lot in common. He was a brilliant canoeist and a clever fisherman, and from him I learned how to travel standing up and pole a canoe, a technique frowned upon by qualified canoe instructors. But sometimes it is the only safe way to navigate tricky water in real wilderness as it enables the canoeist to see more detail in the rapids ahead, and the pole is useful as a brake.

Mostly we talked about techniques for travelling through this wild country. Like me, he marvelled at the variety and profusion of living things on the great granite batholith and wondered why this great wilderness was so well endowed.

Besides being a fine writer Patterson could spin a yarn. I visited him in Victoria and told him about meeting the wolverine on Bald Mountain. He told me that about ten days before Christmas 1929 when he was living in his cabin in the Headless Valley a wolverine had got into his cache and shat all over his supplies. He shot the animal and made it into a stew. Using a couple of enamel plates he put portions of the stew on the roof of the cabin to freeze and continued doing this until he had ten frozen slabs. He then put his bedroll, rifle and axe on his narrow toboggan and set off to walk more than three hundred kilometres down the frozen river to meet Gordon Matthews at the Hudson Bay Post for Christmas. Every night he cut down a dead jack pine, made a huge fire and melted a slab of stew. The trip took him exactly ten days and the temperature, as far as he could tell, stayed well below zero. When I asked him how the wolverine tasted he gave a wry grin and said, 'I sort of reckon I invented TV dinners.'

One of the things we talked about a lot and made us allies was the damming of the Peace River at Hudson's Hope. The government proudly called it 'the biggest dammed lake in the world', and said it would be able to be seen from the surface of the moon. I was very much against the dam and the hydro-electric power plant for I had seen the disastrous effects of the much smaller Australian Snowy Mountains

Scheme. The Canadian plan was to flood the valleys of the Peace, the Finlay and the Parsnip rivers, and in our opinion that would be a mistake.

Occasionally we talked about writing. We both agreed it was not easy and the only way was to continue struggling until one got it right. He said that when writing a book one was always very much alone. I don't think we ever discussed Farson or any of the other writers connected with Vancouver Island. Nearly all our conversations were about animals, canoeing and ways of catching fish. I learned a lot about the outdoors from this old bushman. I remember he always carried a mousetrap in his pack. He set it at the end of a portage overnight and nearly always caught mice for bait. Although he was a fly fisherman he also like to eat char, like bull trout or Dolly Varden, which are easier to catch on bait.

I was beginning to understand all those years ago that isolation was a good thing. Living in a lonely cabin in the wilderness was turning out to be more instructive than teaching in a university in Australia. I had partially understood this some years earlier when I was in Greenland, but I had succumbed to temptation when I returned to King's in London. I had technical toys to play with at the Australian National University. I had an electron microprobe analyser that was capable of counting the number of atoms in a thousandth of a square millimetre of anything and telling me what atoms they were. A fine tool—yet too much. Laboratories cause scientists to think about very small things. Here in Meade's cabin I was doing the reverse. I was thinking about much bigger things and my tools were very simple: a pair of stout boots, a rifle and a fishing rod. True, I was meeting far fewer people, but the ones I did meet were down to earth, and I was running into lots more wild animals.

The most common predator in the region was the cougar and one day, when fishing the Robertson River, which runs into the lake on the southern side, I met one. I was standing in the shallow river just upstream from an old logging trestle, a good place for cutthroat trout. I was working my fly back to me with a left-hand twist, when I saw a cougar that had been following the rail track and had walked on to the bridge. He saw me at the same instant and stopped, one paw poised in the air. I looked at the ten-metre spring that he would have to take to reach me and decided that he wouldn't, and carried on fishing. He realised I was no threat and carried on walking. I discovered later that although these big cats are fine swimmers, they are sensible enough not to attack anything in the water. That was an experience I could never have had in a laboratory.

Vancouver Island has the highest concentration of

North and South America's most widely distributed animal, the cougar. Once, so I was told, the professional cougar hunter Donny Palmer collected the bounty on two hundred cougars in one year just around Cowichan Lake. I'm not sure what the bounty was in the sixties, but Donny probably made quite a good living. Today, it costs several thousand dollars for a permit to hunt a single cougar and one must hunt with a guide and only in the three winter months after the young have left home.

I was lucky enough to go on a cougar hunt with Donny in 1968. It was an accident and it happened like this. I had recently written a column on cougars called 'The Timid Cat'. Also writing for the paper was a woman who told me these big cats were very dangerous and my article was nonsense. She wrote a gossip column and she had asked me to pick up her article when I was on the way to town with my own. As I arrived at her place she screamed that she hoped I had my gun as a cougar had just gone into the barn. I didn't really pay much attention because her children were safely inside the house, but I walked disbelievingly over to the barn just in time to see a cougar slink out through the broken boards in the back. Because I hadn't expected a cougar to be there, I had left my gun in the truck. The gossip columnist must have phoned Donny before my arrival because a few minutes later his yellow truck with the baying hounds in the back came hurtling into the yard.

I grabbed my gun, and Donny and I went on a cougar hunt. But it was a hunt with a difference because Donny wanted to get the bounty on the animal and its skin, and I wanted the cougar to get away. In the long run it did because the hounds couldn't find the trail; they were confused by all the different cat scents in the forest around the house. The woman who lived there didn't like cougars, but she was always putting out food and saucers of milk for stray cats. Oddly, it was the strays that probably attracted the cougar in the first place; when deer are scarce the younger and less experienced of these big cats often prey on small domestic animals.

Standing on top of Bald Mountain soon after I arrived on my first trip I'd had a good view of the lie of the land. As every river in this valley except the Cowichan flowed to the west, clearly there had been a major geological uplift of land which had blocked the flow of westward flowing rivers and caused the large lake to form. Later, the small eastward-flowing Cowichan had cut back and captured the waters of the South Arm and its flow had doubled or tripled in size.

Ever since that day on the mountain my interest has been focussed on the wilder west. The loggers hadn't reached these more remote rivers in 1968, and I got to know the original forest quite well. Mostly, I travelled alone and just talked to the trees, but there were two human sources that I have to acknowledge and couldn't have done without: the shy, isolated Nitinat people and a wonderful wild character everybody called Big Arthur who was so skilled in the harvesting of wildlife he deserves his own book.

When I talked about the uplift of land to the Nitinat who lived right on the coast at Clo-oose much further to the west they told me they knew of this event. It was the coming of the Thunderbird and they told me it happened a few hundred years before the arrival of the white men. There was a giant earthquake and huge tidal waves. They were too polite to say so but I could tell they thought the advent of European civilisation was far worse. To placate the great bird they honoured it with large symbols of a black and red bird at the top of their totem poles and on things like blankets. My more modern view was that two tectonic plates had collided probably less than a thousand years ago and the events dated from roughly that time. I could have written a scientific paper about it but I had much bigger fish to fry. I was fascinated by the tremendous wealth of the land. I wanted to understand why this very acid rock and soil could produce so many animals and fish and so many giant trees. While thinking about it, I went fishing. I had no idea then that forty years later I would be trying to teach this approach to thinking to an eight-year-old.

6

Big Arthur

Big Arthur was completely different from the shy natives of Clo-oose near the far end of Nitinat Lake; he was an extrovert. He liked to explore, and he told me he knew of a place in the west where there were lots of fish but where no people had been before.

'Not even the Nitinat?' I asked.

'Naw,' he said scornfully, 'they hardly ever come inland and they certainly don't move around like I do. They stay put.'

In another world Arthur would have been a star, but he was smart and content to remain in the small village at the head of the lake—the biggest fish in a small pool. Here he was El Supremo, top dog and number-one cat. He also claimed he was number one with the women, but that side of him I didn't see. He was certainly the best pitcher and the top hitter in the baseball team. Most impressive for all of us he was the biggest catcher of fish, and for that he was the talk of the town. People would say, 'Did you see what Big Arthur got today?' Superficially he was an athlete but lurking underneath, hidden from the world, was an intellectual, which was perhaps the reason he and I became friends. He thought fly-fishing a bit silly, and I didn't approve of many of the things he did on the river, for I had learned to fish in a more traditional place, but I remained content to learn from him.

One day when performing some great feat of strength in the forest he casually likened himself to Paul Bunyan and I realised that Bunyan was Arthur's role model. I didn't ask if he never shaved the whiskers from off his horny hide but simply drove them through with a hammer and bit them off inside. I knew what the answer would be, so I just smiled.

Big Arthur could be a pain in the arse to keep up with in the woods, but it was good exercise. The fact that I managed to stay with him perhaps endeared me to the big lug. In addition, I never tried to compete with him. Looking back now, I realise that he probably saw me as his Boswell. He never knew I was struggling to become a writer, but he was smart enough to know the direction I might be travelling in. Sometimes I imagined him in a place like Chelsea or Greenwich Village and I could see him there, no problem at all, except there'd be no fishing.

I don't remember how I met Arthur. It was probably on a Friday night in the village pub. And I don't remember most of the trips we did. I just know he was the biggest fish catcher I ever came across, both in numbers and in size. I have no idea if he is still alive, but I am recording his story here in the hope that someday this piece of paper will be found, because Big Arthur would like to be remembered by fishermen. Of that I am certain.

A short time before Arthur and I met, John Diefenbaker, prime minister of Canada, visited the lake. He was a rather strange man: he used to wear a frock-coat and a deerstalker hat and seemed to be trying to look like Sherlock Holmes. He wasn't the first or the last Canadian politician to dress up. Pierre Trudeau tried to look like Lawrence of Arabia (a man loved and respected by Henry Williamson, but disliked by me) and later the leader of a newer party modelled himself on Tom Cruise and campaigned on a jet ski. Why Canadian politicians feel the need to do this sort of thing is beyond me. Perhaps it has something to do with trying to impress the neighbours to the south, or perhaps they feel that alongside the English unless they dress up they lack sartorial elegance.

Despite the prime minister's odd garb, the logging companies decided to take Dief the Chief (as he loved to be called) fishing. They took him to an unnamed creek a few kilometres to the south-west of Meade's cabin. They needed a helicopter to get there. To the ordinary guy in the village, the place where Dief the Chief had fished became a legend and it was henceforth, the Chief's Hole. It was the local equivalent of Everest—many of us locals simply wanted to reach it because it was there.

I was interested therefore when Big Arthur said he knew how to get to the Chief's Hole, and would I like to go fishing. There was a hitch, of course; we didn't have a helicopter and there was a hell of a hike and some serious climbing to do before we could get at the fish. Arthur had selected me as his partner because I had a lot of rock-climbing gear and a fair bit of climbing experience. He said the only way to get into the canyon without a helicopter was by climbing down an overhanging cliff. He said that if we could get in on that side of the river the fishing would be even better than the place a fair bit lower down on the other bank where the helicopter had taken the Chief.

I was cautious because, although we were both experienced in the bush, when climbing with another person you put your life in his or her hands. Climbing partners have to be chosen very carefully indeed.

Arthur was impatient with me. 'Don't you climbing guys have some special way of going down cliffs?'

'Yes, it's called abseiling, or roping down.'

'Could I do it?'

I smiled to myself. Arthur was built like a sasquatch and was fitter than a marathon runner. 'I imagine so—all you do is put a rope through a carabiner and walk backwards down the cliff.'

'How about getting back up again?'

At this point I had to think. I imagined we would be able to escape by letting the water carry us downstream, a method we called frogging it: half wading and half swimming. But Arthur said no, the water was too fierce and we'd be smashed to pieces. The whole point of getting to this inaccessible spot was that it was a resting place for fish below the falls. To get out we'd have to climb up the cliff again. Jumars hadn't been invented then, or if they had they were yet to reach our neck of the woods, so I had to come up with something else.

'How steep is this cliff?'

'It's vertical for maybe a hundred feet but then it over-hangs for quite a bit at the bottom.'

'Hmm, maybe we could climb out like one does out of a crevasse using Prusik loops.'

It was by no means certain that we would be able to, but the die was cast—we would have to try.

Two days later we set out for the legendary hole.

'It's a good time,' said Arthur. 'Those big hook-nose western coho are running.'

After a lot of driving in my battered old pick-up truck we came to a blaze on a tree. Arthur had left this mark on his exploratory trip, but with my dislike of advertising I would have preferred a signpost that was a little more discreet. We geared up like we were set to scale the North Wall of the Eiger—hundreds of metres of abseil line, slings, carabiners, even a piton or two—but we were also carrying my big bamboo salmon rod and Arthur's bloody great gaff as we set off to walk through the forest. The firs were big, incredibly tall and with huge girths that would need several people arms outstretched to encircle them. Today, because of active logging, many of these trees are gone and lesser species are taking their place.

After a while, through the silence of the forest we could hear the rush of water. Then there was a small clearing and a sudden cliff. We peered over, and there was the river. We could see the falls and the ledge we were making for below. We skirted the cliff, found a convenient place to belay, and dropped the abseil line down to the river.

It was not easy, but we made it. I had my doubts about

climbing out again, but meanwhile there were the fish. The pool was full of huge salmon; I had never seen so many fish in my life. I cast into the main part of the pool, while Arthur followed the ledge around the corner where the current was slacker and the fish were resting. I realised that there it was easier to gaff fish, so that was why he hadn't brought a rod.

Within seconds I had a fish on. I could not believe the awesome power and sheer brutishness of this big male coho. I don't remember how long I fought him, but I do remember becoming very tired. I understood that I was not going to land this fish, and right at that moment the heavy five-metre salmon rod, built of carefully glued triangular pieces of the best quality Tonkin cane, snapped in two. I had never heard of a split cane rod breaking. This is not supposed to happen, but it did. Lots of line was taken from the reel, which was screaming so much I thought it too would break. And then, even though the rushing and roaring noise of the water continued, it seemed there was silence.

I sat down on the sloping rock platform and almost began to weep. After a few minutes of reflection, in which I cursed myself for being an idiot, I laid the broken rod and the now-still reel on the rock and went to look for Big Arthur. The heavy silk line streamed out into the river. Why I didn't wind it in I do not know.

Around the corner Arthur was down on his knees,

gaff held high, poised over the water. At that moment he struck. Leaping to his feet, he hauled in the big gaff. The giant hook was embedded in the side of a huge fish. And stuck in the corner of its mouth was my fly, still attached to my line. I couldn't believe my eyes; I thought that fish had gone forever.

Because the rod had broken and I had lost the fish, there was an ethical question about the way the fish had been caught. Arthur never bothered with finer points and settled it by entering the fish in that year's *Field & Stream* competition, saying that he caught the fish with a fly. This was partially correct—a fly had been used, but not by Arthur.

The fly was an unusual one sent to me from Scotland by my friend Rob Wilson. So the fly Rob considered ideal for big predatory fish, and had called the tiger fly, got the publicity it deserved. I don't remember the exact weight of the fish but it was the second-largest coho ever recorded and the largest caught in fresh water. The world record, only a few grams heavier, came out of salt water.

Ever after in my mind, it was the fish that had behaved the more creditably, compared with us two. I can understand the big male coho deciding to rest after our battle; he just didn't reckon on the streamside smartness of the smartest river man I ever knew: my partner in crime, Big Arthur.

We climbed back up the cliff using nylon slings

attached to the abseil line with Prusik knots. It was a laborious climb, what climbers call a proper throtch, but we made it.

When I was a small child my father, who was a great believer in simple graphic messages, took me to see a painting by William Blake of a lion lying down with a lamb. I thought the idea silly, but as I grew older I began to appreciate what Blake was saying. I've come to see that it's probably a good idea for lambs to cuddle up to lions, for vegetarians to meet hunters, and for rangers to mix with poachers, for there is much each one can learn from the other. Rednecks are not all bad, and greenies aren't all mad. Unfortunately nowadays the pendulum has swung so far in one direction it's only a matter of time before all outdoor activities are prohibited altogether and replaced by video games. I was once told how to kill a bear by somebody who had done it only on a computer.

I suppose it was because I was aware of this danger that I first became involved with Big Arthur. In every respect but one, which was that we both loved to be out in the woods, we were as different as two men can be. I was the ultimate green-neck, and he chewed tobacco and spat out the juice as he gaffed another innocent fish. Arthur committed some terrible sins, or so it seemed to me. He once took nineteen steelhead from the big pool near Steelhead Rock. But now I am able to put these things into perspective. He was an efficient predator, it's true, but not nearly as efficient as a single bear. There were dozens of bears on that same river, catching fish every day. He was also far less efficient than one commercial fishing boat, and there were many of those massed at the mouths of the rivers we fished.

The passing of time has made it clear to me that the enemy is not guys like Big Arthur. His methods were unorthodox, perhaps, but to ban guns and barbs on hooks is similar to prohibiting drink and drugs. It doesn't stop people using them. They just go underground. The answer is education. We need to understand more fully the consequences of our actions and to take responsibility for them, and always be ready to change our minds. The preference too often nowadays is to put someone else in charge, to hand personal decision-making over to officials and guides.

Whatever anybody said about him, Arthur was always able to take responsibility. When I tackled him about the nineteen steelhead and asked him if it were true he said, 'Sure I did it. My family was hungry.' I decided that an honest poacher was a lot better than a two-faced preacher. At least you knew where you were.

So I began to see Arthur's point of view and he began

to see mine. True, he still thought fly-fishing rather silly, and I couldn't bring myself to gaff any fish, but we fished together a lot and got on well. One evening I decided to fish the mouth of the Robertson River where it flowed into Bear Lake. These days, Bear Lake seems no more than a bay off the south side of Cowichan Lake, but then it was separated from the main lake but linked by a channel called the Bear River. I told Arthur I was going to fish the mouth of the Robertson and asked him if he'd like to come. There was a steep drop off there, and I intended to bump a fly down the edge of this sub-aquatic cliff.

I wasn't surprised when he said he'd come, but I was very surprised when he said he wouldn't bring along any tackle.

'No,' he said, 'I don't think I will fish this evening. I'll just watch and see if I can pick up any points on this fly-fishing business.'

I had recently acquired a Chestnut Prospector recommended by my friend Raymond Patterson, and Arthur and I put this large canoe into Bear Lake. Arthur elected to kneel in the front because he wanted to peer into the depths to look for fish. I had good eyes but I knew his were better. If there was anything to be seen in the lake he would spot it first. So, despite the fact that Arthur was heavier than I was and that the canoe was not trimmed correctly, I agreed.

Fortunately for the stability of the craft there was only one paddle, and, being the leader in this particular situation, I took the canoe across the ripple-free surface of the lake. I was using the Indian stroke in which the paddle never comes out of the water, and the canoe soon reached the mouth of the river. It was the first time Arthur had seen me paddle a canoe. I could tell he was impressed.

'I thought you had to keep changing sides to make these things go straight,' he said.

I'd begun trailing my heavy silk line when we took off from the shore—not really trolling, as Arthur thought, but just giving the ungreased line a good soaking before we reached the river. When we reached the drop-off, I cast towards the mouth and let my fly—a small size-10 Silver Doctor attached to the line by a short but stout leader— bounce along the bottom.

This fly in the larger sizes, which have lower numbers, is commonly used for Atlantic salmon. Mine had just arrived in the post from Scotland, sent by Robert Wilson. Rob's version of the fly had a flat silver tinsel body ribbed with oval silver wire. The wings were made of strips of swan or goose feather dyed red, yellow and green. The hackle was a bright blue cock's feather and the tail was a golden pheasant tippet. Rob said he thought the fly was one of the best he had come across for Scottish sea trout and should work well for big trout in Canada.

Because the slope was quite steep I waited longer between each bounce to allow the fly to sink back towards the bottom. I could see that Arthur was watching my technique intently, and although he was not fishing he reminded me of a heron. I was seeing a new side to my friend: he was more patient, less bull-at-a-gate-like, than usual.

I must have made thirty or forty casts into pretty much the same place, allowing for the drift of the canoe, when I got a strike, and what a strike it was. It was immediately apparent I was into a very strong fish, and the canoe started to move out into the lake. Arthur's placid attitude immediately changed. He became excited and started giving shouts of encouragement, which I did my best to ignore. The canoe moved with increasing speed and this fish, this magnificent unseen fish, took the two of us—more than ninety kilograms of Arthur, perhaps eighty of me plus another thirty-five kilos of canoe and gear—on a Nantucket sleigh ride. Neither Arthur nor I had ever experienced anything like it.

This continued for twenty minutes, and then we saw the fish. It was now making tighter and tighter circles, getting nearer and nearer to the boat with each circuit, and we could see its mammoth size and the Silver Doctor almost straightened out in the corner of the fish's mouth. It was swimming peculiarly, somewhat on one side. Neither of us thought that was because of the fight. There was something odd about this giant fish.

We had no landing net, and even if we'd had a typical trout net it wouldn't have been big enough, but Arthur reckoned he could lift the fish into the canoe if I could get it close enough. I knew that if anyone could scoop that fish out of the water without any gear it would be Arthur, so I told him I would do my best. After what seemed like another ten minutes I brought the fish to the canoe's right-hand side and Arthur's strong right arm plunged into the water as fast as a grizzly bear's. His hand went into the gills and the fish was in the boat.

The first thing I heard from Arthur was a cry of repugnance and horror, for fixed onto the right side of the fish was a lamprey thirty-five centimetres long. It immediately fell off the flapping fish and my friend attacked the long brown seemingly finless eel-like creature with his knife. I thought for a moment that in his passion he would stab a hole through the canoe bottom, but instead he sprayed my fine craft with gallons of lamprey blood and chopped up the ugly parasitic fish.

The trout was a beautiful cutthroat, the biggest we had ever seen. Neither of us believed they got that big.

'I have to admit,' said Arthur, 'I was wrong about this fly-fishing caper; there's something in it after all. Who would have thought a giant bastard like this sucker would have fallen for such an itty-bitty fly. You have to get this one stuffed.' He paused for a minute and then said, 'You know this bastard fought like hell; just think how it would have fought if that fucking lamprey hadn't been sucking its blood.'

I hadn't thought of that; in fact it had never occurred to me that lampreys came into Cowichan Lake. Nor had I ever thought of getting a fish stuffed. I'd always regarded fish as food, and had assumed that Arthur thought the same. But I remembered his commercial connections (he made a secret orange bait paste out of borax and fish eggs and sold it to tackle dealers) and realised there was a business side to fishing that I hadn't thought about very much.

When we returned to the village the fish went on view for all to see, and we weren't at all secretive about where we got it for almost everybody fished Bear Lake. Everyone who saw the fish urged me to get it stuffed.

I wonder now why I ever allowed them to influence me. I think it was just another example of my uncertainty about myself at that time. Today I would reject the whole idea of preserving a dead fish to nourish my ego, but back then I went along with the crowd. The fish had to be frozen and then taken to Campbell River where the nearest taxidermist was. To put the whole thing in perspective, let me say I no longer remember how long the fish was or how much it weighed. I only remember Arthur's horror, the length of the lamprey and three other things. First, it cost I think a dollar, or maybe two dollars, an inch to have the fish set up, and it took me nearly two years to save enough money so I could go and pick it up. Second, the fish was on display for over a year in the Campbell River tackle shop complete with a brass plate that gave the name of the taxidermist but said nothing about the angler. Third, and this was the big thing for me, Roderick Haig-Brown who lived in Campbell River and was the most celebrated angler in North America looked at it, took his pipe out of his mouth and muttered something about knowing fish like that were out there and wishing he could connect up with one soon.

Years later when I was living on Cortes Island, which lies between Vancouver Island and the mainland, an old German who tied the most awful flies and who had built a tourist 'castle' nearby out of concrete blocks asked me if he could hang the fish he had found abandoned in my barn inside his banqueting room. So I gave it to him. I heard later that he had stuck one of his crudely tied flies in the fish's lower lip and was telling his visitors that he had caught it on that fly in the local lake. He then sold them some of his flies. I knew then I should have eaten that fish.

Since that time I have always been very sceptical about the pictures in fishing magazines and the people who go on about the size or the weight of a fish, and I remind myself of the beauty of fish. For some reason, most people think of birds as beautiful but not fish, and for a long time I have been trying to work out why.

Years before I went to live in Meade's cabin I remember being amazed at the colours of fish, especially the char I had caught in the Arctic watersheds of the far north and the sticklebacks I caught as a child in the Cranberry Brook in England. But then I recalled how the colours of the fish rapidly faded as they died and that was why I started to put them back. We have an expression about awkwardness, 'like a fish out of water', and now I realise it applies to beauty too. That beauty fades so quickly when a fish is removed from its element. So these days, if I am lucky enough to hook a beautiful brook trout, like I sometimes do in the misnamed Rainbow Lake in the Snowy Mountains, unless I am camping and hungry I admire it for a second or two and let it go. Photographs never do fish justice, so nowadays I mainly use my camera to record places rather than the fish I catch.

Many more years have passed and I am still writing about things the human species has difficulty with. I have never claimed to know any of the answers, but I think I am getting better at asking the right questions. If we want our planet and our species to survive, doesn't it make sense for all of us to use less of everything and consider more carefully the way we behave?

7

The Secret Coast

One of the attractions of living in Meade's cabin in the sixties was the easy access to Vancouver Island's wild west coast. As the logging progressed so rapidly west of Cowichan Lake it became possible to reach the Nitinat River on logging roads, and possession of a canoe opened up all sorts of wonderful country.

Even today, in the second decade of the twenty-first century, there is still no road along the west coast of Vancouver Island and this wildness continues northwards beyond the island for thousands of kilometres. True, a road now runs from Victoria at the southern tip of the island towards the town of Port Renfrew, but that road was not cheap to construct because it crosses numerous rivers that were difficult to bridge. North of there on the west coast there is no road at all to the top of the island. Fortunately Vancouver Island, like most of British Columbia, still has one of the wildest and most unspoilt coasts in the world, and even in the increasingly populous south there are still many lonely lakes and wild rivers to explore.

Today, part of this beautiful coast can be accessed at Long Beach. Wolves and bears are common here. To give you an idea how wild it is, recently a university student asleep in his sleeping-bag on the sand was rudely awoken early one morning by a she-wolf dragging the bag with him in it towards her two hungry cubs. When he wriggled out of the bag the three wolves quickly vanished. They were obviously used to investigating flotsam that ended up on the lonely beach.

Not far from that point there is an isolated luxury hotel where my wife and I were treated to a stay a few years ago. It has to be one of the world's most spectacularly situated hotels. Recently, I read an essay by Tim Flannery describing his visit to this wild coast and how he was awestruck by the sheer abundance of life. He used the word *titanic* to describe it, and said it was almost beyond his reckoning. It is indeed a giant world. Go there if you like unspoilt beauty but take only photographs and leave nothing behind.

At the northern tip of the island is the remote and wild Cape Scott, and just to the east is the entrance to Queen Charlotte Strait. Nowadays it is possible to follow the protected Inside Passage south of the cape but Captain James Cook, although he recorded an inlet there in 1778, had no time to explore it. He was trying to find a new route back to England but, needing repairs, he was finally forced to turn south-west and sail back to Hawaii, where he was killed.

Cook's former lieutenant George Vancouver was sent to survey the waters between the island and the mainland. In his log book Vancouver, who grew up sailing the difficult waters of the English Wash, called these Canadian waters 'one of the vilest stretches of water in the world'. In addition to rapids in the sea and massive whirlpools he also had to contend with the huge and dangerous underwater mountain called Ripple Rock that even at the highest tide came within two metres of the surface and blocked the passage. His guiding of the *Discovery* in 1792 through that nozzle-shaped narrow strait now called Discovery Passage must rank as one of the greatest pieces of sailing ever.

In 1958, the Canadian government finally managed to blow the top off this giant underwater peak in one of the greatest non-nuclear explosions ever, and this made the route passable for modern ships. Large craft were slow to take advantage of this new way north but nowadays cruise ships are starting to use this spectacular route along the west coast. However, if one travels north of Vancouver Island along the coast of the mainland to see the wildlife, one needs a small boat to poke into the inlets and travel close to the shore. It is one of the most contorted coasts in the world and although it is now accurately charted most of it is never visited.

When I eventually left Meade's cabin I found a small sailboat, the *Northern Maid*, that would be my new home. Gaff-rigged with cotton sails and no engine, she was seven metres long including her fixed bowsprit, and built of cedar over oak with spars of the finest spruce. She was just big enough to live on and I bought her because I wanted to see more of this incredible coast. There was another 16,000 kilometres of British Columbia coastline north of Vancouver Island and there were no roads.

I never succeeded in seeing all of it but I visited many rivers and inlets that might never have been entered before. As I suspected, wild animals became much easier to see the further I sailed away from civilisation. Each day I travelled towards the north everything got better and better. This mountainous area with all its rich rivers was so good to me that I felt at last I was beginning to grasp the secret of life. My little boat with her full-length keel slowly made her way towards Cape Saint Elias and, as we journeyed together, we went backwards in time.

As there are so many rivers pouring off the mountains into the sea on the western part of this longest of all coastlines, the water close to the land is still largely fresh, so a supply of fresh water was never a problem.

Inside I had a small cast-iron stove I cooked on, and I burned bark and driftwood that I picked up on the beach. I spent the time slowly sailing up the coastline living in a space so small I had to slide back the hatch to pull my pants on every morning.

Living on a boat was the obvious way to find out more about the salmon. Mostly I stood on the bowsprit hanging on to the forestay and watching the salmon getting out of the way of the bow. As I sailed north I spent many hours looking down into the sea where the salmon were smelling their way home. Sometimes I would follow them into rivers, anchor near the mouth, then take my canoe and follow the fish upstream to watch them spawn.

To modern sailors reading this I should explain that this old-style sloop had two headsails but was not a cutter because she had a fixed bowsprit. Heavy for her length she carried a lot more sail than a boat of that small size does today because she was designed when few could afford a motor. Her hull had a full-length keel, which made her hard to get going but once moving she would continue much longer than a modern boat. When there was no wind I moved her around harbours using the tiller and the single sweep. In the more popular harbours of Vancouver Island, richer yachtsmen were full of admiration for the way she continued to sail when according to them there was no wind at all. To my way of thinking older boats based on working fishing boats are much more practical for cruising than those based on boats designed to race.

I didn't understand the mystery of the huge numbers of Pacific salmon but it seemed no one else did either. Atlantic salmon were far less numerous and had never been common even in Roman times. These fish on the west coast of the Pacific were very different indeed; there were so many of them. Something inside told me the steelhead was the important clue, but although I was learning to trust my instincts I still needed more facts. I marvelled at the wonderful water around me and wondered if the fish could survive the disappearance of the trees.

I still remember the day when quite suddenly I understood what was happening. I had had to sail with salmon for nearly a year before it finally clicked. On the batholith, I had seen countless millions of them die on spawning, and on these dying salmon the giant grizzly bears fed by hooking them out of the rivers with their long curved claws. The bear would take usually just a single bite behind the salmon's head and drop it somewhere near the edge of the forest. Then the wolves dragged some of the fish off and ate too. Then came the eagles and ravens, the shorter clawed black bears, and hundreds of other creatures that picked clean the bones. Nature never wasted a single thing. The really large trees were nearly always close to the rivers for the bears during spawning season didn't travel very far into the woods and so neither did the nutrients from the fish.

This was the hidden secret: the fish fed everything. When they died they supplied nutrients to everything else. It was as clear as the nose on anyone's face. The fish, full of alkali elements such as calcium, supported the acid land. In autumn the rivers clogged up with dead and stinking fish which were actually bringing in the alkali elements from the deep ocean and it was this that made the Coast Range Batholith so different from the acid granite of Australia.

Here in British Columbia, the greatest batholith of all was able to support the world's largest biomass because of anadromous fish that died on spawning. The giant trees, the profuse wildlife and huge bears were all here because of the deaths of countless billions of salmon.

My little gaff rigger, only four times as long as I was,

made a fine place to live because she was small enough to be easy to maintain. At low water she stood completely upright on her long keel and I could scrub and paint the lower part of her hull during a change of the tide. I did that often because a boat with a clean bottom sails like a bird. The *Northern Maid* was so well balanced that once the sails were adjusted she didn't need a helmsman. I was living closer to nature than I had been when I was in Greenland or in Meade's cabin at the lake. I didn't see other humans for nearly a year, but I saw many other animals every day. There are almost no settlements on the wild and rugged west coast of Canada's most beautiful province and I sailed alone through waters full of salmon, otters and killer whales close to a great land covered in trees and full of bears.

Travelling on the plane from Sydney to Vancouver there were only a dozen passengers like me. The rest of the seats were taken up by a huge tour group of Australians mainly from inland country towns who spoke excitedly of their forthcoming trip to Alaska, although they were actually spending most of their time travelling through the Rocky Mountains of British Columbia and Alberta. Their route was the popular twenty-first-century one: up the Fraser Canyon along the Icefields Parkway from Banff to Jasper then across to Prince

George and then following the highway north to the big city of Anchorage and then coming back to Vancouver on the ferry via the Inside Passage. They said they couldn't wait to get to Alaska to see the Kodiak bears. I told the old farmer I was talking to that he would see lots of bears everywhere, especially on the coast, but he firmly told me the Kodiaks were the biggest of all and they only occurred in Alaska and that would be the highlight of his trip.

I didn't disillusion him and tell him that in reality, in North America there are only three bears, just as in the fairytale. They are black, brown and white. The smaller, generally more dangerous and sneaky black bear can be any of those three colours. It is only this bear *Ursus americanus* that is exclusively North American. Brown bears (usually known as grizzlies) are widely distributed throughout the northern hemisphere and are found in Spain and Norway as well as right across Europe and Asia. Probably due to population pressure brown bears migrated to America like everyone else. The white polar bear has a smaller range but is also found further north.

The present day confusion about bears is due to a misguided American, Clinton Hart Merriam, who never visited the habitats yet classified common brown bears into more than eighty-four different species based on skulls sent to him by American hunters. In 1947, after

Merriam died, the distinguished American biologist Victor H. Cahalane, not wanting to be critical of the great man, politely said, 'Probably no piece of research has brought dignified mammalogists nearer to name-calling and nose-punching than the question of correctly identifying the grizzly bears.' Sadly Taronga Park Zoo in Sydney and people like Alaskan moose hunter Sarah Palin continue to perpetuate the Kodiak myth. Scientists search for truth, but for too many people today advertising and amassing money matter more.

The world is full of surprises, perhaps because we tend to focus on the first thing that impresses us. Many Australians who think of Canada as a cold place are surprised when I tell them there are deserts with tumbleweed and rattlesnakes in British Columbia. English visitors are surprised to find that in summer southern Vancouver Island which they had been told was like England in climate is often more like Spain. Canada is generally thought of as being covered in ice and snow and full of people riding on sledges. Certainly it is like that in some places but it has considerable climatic diversity. It is also a vast empty land like Australia with roughly the same low population density.

Canada has fifty per cent more people than Australia but it is half as big again with more time zones than any other country except Russia, which it resembles by having lots of snow and people dressed in fur hats. The big difference between Canada and Russia though is water; the northern Pre-Cambrian Shield is somewhat lopsided and gently undulating so Canada has many millions of lakes, which hold over half the world's fresh water, whereas flatter Russia has mainly swamps and bogs. Canada's coastline is the world's longest at 200,000 kilometres, and most of the great rivers run 'down north' into the Arctic Ocean or Hudson Bay and were major routes in the early fur-trading days. Canada has always moved huge amounts of its natural resources by water and has always had a large mercantile marine fleet. Even now, around its own coast, it is still one of the world's most maritime nations.

Along the Inside Passage and towards the north on the west coast are a series of red-painted government wharves built to serve the public and for boats in transport to load and deposit goods. Most are still free much to the amazement of visiting Americans. That is why I was able to live on my boat and visit the north with relatively little cash. The west coast though, apart from a few isolated settlements, is still as wild as the day Cook landed at Nootka and claimed the coast for England more than two hundred and thirty years ago.

8

How to Fillet a Fish

I used to go to the western edge of the southern part of the island when I lived in Meade's cabin in 1968 because of another amenity, the remote West Coast Trail. The trail was built during the last days of sail early in the twentieth century by the government to help shipwrecked mariners who had come to grief attempting to enter the Strait of Juan de Fuca after crossing the Pacific.

One of the world's most dangerous coasts, that stretch was known as the Graveyard of the Pacific, and many square-rigged ships, as well as some steam-driven craft, were driven onto its lee shore. There were more than a hundred wrecks. The government cut a walking trail through the great forest running south along the top of the cliffs towards Victoria, and built a shelter cabin about every thirty kilometres. They also rigged a crude telephone line attached to the giant trees, and in each cabin there was a box where one wound a handle in order to generate enough current to ring the coastguard to the south. Cables were strung across the numerous rivers, some with metal passenger baskets so survivors could follow the wire to meet rescuers.

After the advent of radar in the early forties there were far fewer wrecks and by the sixties the trail had been abandoned for years. I reached it at Tsusiat Falls by paddling my canoe part of the way down Nitinat Lake, then up the Hobiton River into Hobiton Lake from where I shouldered the canoe and cut a portage to Tsusiat Lake. I paddled across that and then down the Tsusiat River until I reached the falls getting out quickly before they poured over the cliff into the sea. There I left the canoe and walked north along the beach. I then had access to many unfished rivers where I caught salmon and steelhead.

In an effort to save this empty area of wild country from complete destruction by the logging companies I wrote articles describing its virtues and calling it first the Nitinat Triangle and at other times 'Vancouver Island's Own Lake District'. I began writing about the beauties of this wilderness and the magnificence of the West Coast Trail in order to encourage people to go there. The Sierra Club in California became interested and they asked me for photographs, notes and sketch maps of the area, which they turned into a guidebook.

During the next few years people from all over the world started coming to walk the trail and it is now perhaps the most popular wild trail in North America. I am somewhat resentful about this and I no longer respect those people from California because my work and the photographs I supplied were used but I was never acknowledged. The popularity of the trail and the crowded bays and new campsites wrecked the place for me as well as for the few native people of the area. However I believe that the number of hikers is now limited, and one good thing did come out of it: the forest on the west coast was partially saved and the trail is now part of the surviving wilderness Pacific Rim National Park Reserve.

It is also true to say that influential people like Robert F. Kennedy Jr are using their money and power in an attempt to save the whole of British Columbia's beautiful west coast. The popular name for the coast now is the Great Bear Rainforest after a wonderful book of photographs by Ian and Karen McAllister written by Cameron Young that was published in 1997. The McAllisters pointed out that although the coast is clearly a World Heritage area many parts of it were still being logged. I cannot understand why more people don't protest about the killing of something that takes more than a thousand years to grow. I can only suppose it is because most of them live in cities and have never seen anything like it. Few people seem to recognise that all these wonderful life forms are connected and that there is a reason for everything.

The natives of the west coast are quite different from the east-coast Salish at the mouth of the Cowichan River. One of their villages, Clo-oose, was just south of the Nitinat Gap where at one time all the waters of this southern part of Vancouver Island had emptied into the sea. Perhaps I related to them well because, although they had been hit by many of the white man's diseases, they seemed completely independent in their thought and uncorrupted by the white man's culture. They were isolated because there was no road.

I once asked the people who lived at Clo-oose and who netted the mouth of the Hobiton River for its sockeye salmon if they ever went further up the river into the two upper lakes, but all they said was, 'Why?'

It was an old lady from Clo-oose who taught me how to fillet a fish. I met her one day when the sockeye were running and she had caught probably over a hundred in her net. Sockeye return from the ocean in July and spend less time in rivers than any other salmon. They only spawn in river systems that run out of lakes with sandy beaches. They bury their eggs on the beach and die almost immediately.

Sockeye are the best salmon to eat. When I asked the old lady how she knew when to set her nets she told me she could always tell by looking at the moon. She said the salmon did it too and that they always began their run halfway through the seventh moon. She had little English but while we talked she filleted dozens of fish at lightning speed. She went so fast I begged her to slow down so I could see what she was doing but, laughing merrily, she went even faster. Then towards the end she relented and showed me how to do it.

She worked on a piece of cedar sloping at forty-five degrees towards the water. In one smooth movement she gutted the fish and pierced a hole near the tail slipping her finger through while holding the knife horizontally. She then pulled the fish upwards against the knife-edge, and a perfect fillet fell onto the pile. Then she flipped it over and did the other side. She tossed the head and the skin into the water and rinsed her hands. Because of that lesson, most anglers these days think I am very skilful with my fish knife but I will never be as good as the old lady, the fastest fish filleter I ever saw.

Now, years later I realise she must have thought it odd that a man would be interested in small things like salmon, for the men she knew didn't bother with fish. They hunted whales.

The Nitinat people like the other west-coasters to the north built their culture around the migration of the grey whale. The men hunted the whales using large dugout cedar canoes and harpoons, while the women set their nets for salmon. I was exploring a part of the coast well away from the government trail when I stumbled into an area where these people left their dead. They put them in trees. Out of respect for this traditional practice I circled around the area and climbed down onto the beach where I figured I could move north without trespassing on the site.

The northern end of the beach appeared blocked by a headland, but it was low tide and on closer inspection I found I could pass through a tunnel-like cave into a hidden cove. The trouble was it proved impossible to get out of this second cove except by climbing up a fault line to the top of the cliff. This, I hoped, would lead north of the place where I had seen the bodies. Halfway up the climb I found another cave so I crawled in, took the matches out of my pocket and lit one to look around.

The floor of the cave was covered in human bones,

but there were no skulls. Up against the wall were three or four beautiful chests, each about a metre long and made out of broad planks of cedar. Three corners of each chest were bent, by cutting a V first, and the fourth corner was laced together with spruce root. Inside each of these chests were about a dozen male skulls that I thought probably belonged to the crews of whaling canoes. Although not keen on caves, especially ones like this, I crawled through another hole at the back of the first cave where I found whaling harpoons made of strong and heavy Pacific yew and tipped with mussel shell. They were still attached to ropes plaited from cedar bark.

I realised I was probably directly below the bodies in the trees so I retraced my steps disturbing things as little as possible and decided to return south to my canoe. I hadn't got to the river I was trying to reach, but I had discovered a lot more about a proud people—my often neglected and misunderstood western neighbours.

I have found that if we move slowly there is always something we can learn in a human relationship, but it is just as important to pay attention to things most people dismiss as not being particularly communicative, like the great mountains, the rivers and the trees. One develops this skill by doing things alone and unencumbered with unnecessary gear.

I know this is completely against modern practice, but the experts who write books on 'survival' seem to me to carry an awful lot of unnecessary stuff. I meet people walking around the shore of Sydney Harbour where I live wearing climbing boots covered with elastic cuffs to keep out the scree, a couple of ski poles to help them with the hills and of course the obligatory water bladder, something I have never carried in my life probably because all that extra weight makes you sweat.

Most of the equipment I recognise; it's hard not to these days as people now are walking billboards, worse than a commercial break in a TV drama. The problem is there are so many names. It is consumer overkill and I am not sorry some of these companies are now starting to have a difficult time. It is understandable that if a craftsperson or an artist makes something useful and beautiful that they want to put their name on it. In the past this was done discreetly, many of the greats didn't really need to do it, but now the urge to advertise has gone too far; everyone wearing a T-shirt has been conned into promoting somebody else's product. Even the ground of a cricket oval is covered with ads. When I was a kid you got paid for wearing a sandwich board, but now the consumer pays for the privilege of displaying advertising on pretty well every article of clothing. I hope it doesn't last.

I think back to my boyhood when I went everywhere with just a potato, a knife and a box of matches in my pocket. My heroes were the real professionals—we called them tramps. Unlike me they didn't have a home to go to yet they travelled light. Everything they had was tied up in a red bandanna on the end of a stick and carried over one shoulder. They were the 'gentlemen of the road'. The art of travelling light is simple if you throw away anything you don't use. If you do it often enough you will be like the first Australians who always knew the way.

I had been living in Meade's cabin for nearly two years, but I was spending more and more of my time on that wild western shore. I knew about James Cook of course, the first man to chart the St Lawrence River in eastern Canada and the man who showed General Wolfe the way up to the Plains of Abraham enabling the British to take Quebec from the French. He was also the first to chart this coast and had actually landed at Nootka and met the wonderful whale-hunting people.

I wondered about Francis Drake as it was almost certain he had also landed in the area much earlier. His voyage, the first successful circumnavigation of the globe, had been a secret one and the records were concealed by the Crown. However there were stories of how, after he had captured two Spanish treasure ships further south, his ship was so low in the water that in order to complete the circumnavigation he was forced to bury the looted gold near the southern end of what later became known as Vancouver Island.

There is an old story about two hunters lost and out of ammunition on the southern part of the island stumbling through the bush and discovering some steps leading down to a cave. The cave had a huge locked door made out of the distinctive English oak. They intended to return with tools to try and break in, but it was 1939. Both went off to fight and only one survived. After the war the hunter was unable to find his way back to the cave.

There are lots of mysteries in this part of the world and one of the biggest is the identity of Juan de Fuca. Supposedly a Greek who worked for the Spanish he is believed to have reported the strait between the Olympic Peninsula in Washington State and the southern end of Vancouver Island in 1592, but Drake had been there before him in July 1579 looking for a north-west passage. Later Drake's log books were supposedly lost by the Crown. It is amazing that all the later sailors missed this strait, particularly James Cook, the greatest navigator of all. The charts he made were so accurate they are still used today.

Even for the modern sailor, the west coast of Vancouver Island and the Strait of Juan de Fuca are difficult waters. But a great cruising ground is reached at the south-eastern end of the strait where there is a huge inland sea with its southern part in the United States and the northern part in Canada. It is here that ocean-going ships can access Canada's largest western port, Vancouver, and America's largest north-western port, Seattle. Thus, the Strait of Juan de Fuca, in modern times, carries a huge amount of traffic.

The most popular place for small craft in western North America has always been around the islands of the inland sea. The Americans call theirs the San Juan Islands and the Canadians refer to their share as the Gulf Islands. The two nations once fought a war over them, called the Pig War because somebody shot someone else's pig. Fortunately, it was the only casualty but Canada lost a fair bit of its territory.

When I acquired my gaff-rigged sloop with its two headsails I moored her at the public wharf in the tiny port of Sidney just north of British Columbia's capital, Victoria. I got to know the craft first by sailing her south into the fairly busy

American waters of Puget Sound and then back up into the Canadian waters of the Strait of Georgia. This area is a sailor's paradise because it's easy sailing and there are many fine harbours and several hundred islands to explore. It is completely different from the west coast. My plan was to become so familiar with the boat that I could operate her in pitch darkness without thinking. Finally, when I knew the boat and she knew me, we sailed north together through Desolation Sound, the world's most dangerous waters, and into Queen Charlotte Strait, and I looked at the Pacific Ocean's tricky lee shore.

The mountains and the tides to the north had terrified Drake and scared Cook in their square-rigged craft, but an old remittance man called Grey Hill, who lived on an ancient and strangely painted motor cruiser called the *Cape Saint Elias*, admired my little sloop. He told me my smart little sailboat could easily reach the mythical place after which his boat was named. He hadn't been there but he seemed to know a lot about British Columbia's coast. With modern charts, he said, anything was possible with a small seaworthy sailing vessel like mine. He wore heavy glasses and was almost blind but legend had it he knew more about the coast than anyone else, so I thought it was a good sign when he said I should have a go. The important thing, he said, was to always have an alternative plan. After my voyage, the old curmudgeon told me he meant anyone with sense would know it would be easier to beat across the ocean to Japan.

During my time in the northern waters most days I fished for salmon in the sea. The great chinook salmon did not interest me much although I have hooked them and been towed by them more than once. The most fun fish, as well as being one of the best to eat, was the smaller coho. I took a lot of these aboard my little ship by trolling, towing behind the boat, a torpedo-shaped pink wooden plug about ten centimetres long called a Lucky Louie. It wriggled like a mad thing, didn't need to be made to look alive by the angler and was almost irresistible to the fish. But I only did this when I was very hungry.

Whenever I could, I would catch the coho casting a fly. Never though did I catch as large a coho as the one I hooked, and Big Arthur landed, on that fateful day at the waterfall.

9

The Arrival of Ned

Like most old men, I am at my best in the mornings. So after deciding it must now be Wednesday and having spent a couple of days thinking about things that happened in the past, I was hoping that my grandson's arrival would bring me back into the ever-present now. I knew it was difficult for families with young children to get started early in the morning, so I remained patient. I am not sure now what time they did arrive, but I was sitting on the veranda writing about the coast in my notebook when I heard the sound of someone coming down the trail. I felt quite nervous about the meeting. I closed the small black book, slipped the elastic around the cover and put it in my pocket. I crossed the bridge over the gully and started walking towards the place where they would have left the car.

Ned was ahead and obviously excited, but when we met and my son Matthew introduced us he was really quite shy. Ned had blue eyes with a hint of green, fair hair and a slight figure. He was like his father had been, a bit short for his age, probably about a metre tall. In his right hand was a small fishing rod about the same length as he was.

Shyness, I supposed, was a normal reaction, and suddenly I was transported back to my first meeting with my soldier grandfather: I was the first grandchild and a lot younger than Ned when my parents became reconciled with my father's parents, but I do remember I was the reason for the reconciliation. It was early one Sunday morning and my giant grandfather had not yet shaved. He picked me up, rubbed his rough cheek against mine and roared with laughter at my adverse reaction. He was a huge man and he had an odd sense of humour.

Now, with Ned, I decided the best thing was to simply say hello and that it was good to see him.

'Show me the fish Grandpa,' said Ned.

'We need to look at the cabin and dump your other gear first,' I replied.

When we got to the cabin there was great excitement. Ned pointed out that it was made of larger than usual logs.

He caused me to look at the whole structure with new eyes; in my mind it was just a cabin, a place to stay for a night or two, but I suddenly realised it was a large log house. The logs were thirty centimetres or more in diameter and there was a feeling of spaciousness once we were inside. Ned measured himself against them. He was just over three logs high.

I hadn't noticed the size of the logs before, because I was so jet-lagged when I arrived. Four large logs, about two and a half metres above the floor and five metres apart, ran across the huge living room. Beyond the third log there was a wall reaching to the roof. The end of the cabin was screened off to form four bedrooms, two up and two down. Each bedroom had four bunks and there were also a couple of beds. There was so much for a boy to explore; outside there were things like the woodshed and the pit toilet to examine as well. It was every boy's dream, as well as mine.

In the centre of the cabin was a big metal-box stove designed to heat the whole area. Ned peered into the stove, turned and looked back through the open door to the wood-shed. I knew he was thinking about the amount of wood it would use. He inspected the small open kitchen area at one end near the veranda, and the two downstairs bedrooms at the far end, saving to last the best of all: the ladders to the upstairs bunkrooms.

I could tell Ned was impressed. He was thrilled when I

told him he could have the first choice of where to sleep. He climbed all the ladders, tested all the beds and bunks, and eventually chose a top bunk upstairs at the far right-hand end of the cabin.

'Will this one be all right, Grandpa?' he asked.

'Yes, it is the best bunk in the house,' I replied. It was the one I would have chosen myself at his age.

When we got down to ground level again, I told him that living in the woods was different from living in the city because things were so much simpler. Here we concentrated on the most important things in life, like catching fish and not falling into the river. He wanted to rush off and see the river, but I told him that to go near a river first you had to have the right hat. We talked about hats for a while and he said they helped keep you warm and dry. I said that was true, but also pointed out that because of the way light was refracted through water, a light colour, particularly if it was high up, could scare away the fish. Then I pulled out a selection of old hats from my swag and allowed him to choose one. He picked the best one. He took special care to pick a nondescript hat, dark green to blend in with the forest, with a small brim so it wouldn't get in the way of his casting. I could tell he was a quick learner.

'Now,' he said, 'can we go down to the river?'

We could, I said, but when we were within about six

metres of the river's edge we would have to move slowly, rather like a deer does when it is browsing, because fast movements also scare the fish.

So Ned and I set off for the river, leaving Matthew back at the cabin. We moved the whole way through the woods like a couple of ancient mountain men, keeping low, crouching at times, and turning our toes slightly inward in the kind of walk that the mountain men learned from the natives. We were always careful to glide, as jerky movements were not acceptable to the wildlife around us, and we were extremely careful not to get entangled in the spiky devil's club.

Our 'stalk' to the river took a little longer than perhaps it needed to. We didn't see any wild animals, probably because it was the wrong time of day, but we were well satisfied because the few hundred metres we had to travel to reach the water were covered with great skill.

We stopped, as all good anglers should, six metres away from the water—the exact length of Dame Juliana Berners' stiff and heavy fishing rod. I explained to Ned how she would have fished and that fishing for us was absolutely impossible. The little chap nodded his head wisely.

'The water is so fierce today, Grandpa, there is a good chance that the abbess would be washed away,' he said.

We stood looking at the river, listening to its roar, for

what seemed like a full five minutes, and I was impressed with the way Ned took it all in. He seemed thoughtful for his age and able to concentrate, and I thought this was a good sign. I felt pretty sure then—although fishing would be difficult for some time, and we only had a few days—that he would catch a fish.

We walked upstream to the big canyon, to where I thought the young man visiting from Mexico had launched his rubber raft. I tried to understand why anyone would attempt to travel down a river in this condition, but it was beyond my comprehension. I concluded that many of us had become disconnected from nature, although I wasn't sure why. A lot of things puzzled me these days, so I patted my grandson on the shoulder and suggested we should return to the cabin. The smart little chap agreed.

On the way back, we talked a lot about living in the woods, and he seemed remarkably sensible for an eight-year-old. Maybe Matthew had told him that he should listen to his grandfather, but I don't think that was so; instead it seemed to me he had the same kind of curiosity I'd had as a child. I decided that probably all eight-year-olds were like this to some extent, although I couldn't remember much about his father at that age at all. Perhaps the problems I was having at that time with my marriage had interfered with my relationship with my son and now nature was giving

FISHING THE RIVER OF TIME

me a second chance. At any rate, whatever it was we talked about as we walked back from the river was good for both of us and we arrived at the cabin with an appetite for lunch.

Food, perhaps because it is harder to get and more difficult to prepare, always tastes better in the bush. If things had gone according to plan we would have been eating salmon or at the very least a trout, but as my father, Ned's great-grandfather, used to say, the red gods hadn't smiled. I suddenly flashed back to following my father carrying his double-barrelled shotgun through the English woods and me walking three paces behind him like a trained gundog. It was during the Great Depression. I thought perhaps I should mention this to Ned, but in the end I decided just to write it down in my notebook.

I noticed Ned watching me closely. He was too polite to ask what I was writing about, and I decided his parents were doing an excellent job bringing him up. He was cheeky like his father was as a kid, but more polite. Or perhaps I am more tolerant.

Our lunch was a hearty one: long, crusty loaves, plentiful butter and excellent cheese and, most thrilling for me, real root beer. Australia nowadays has probably the world's best ginger beer but North America has root beer and the really good stuff is not found anywhere else.

During the afternoons for the last year or so I have got

into the habit of taking a short nap. There were plenty of interesting things close to the cabin for Ned and Matthew to do without me. Kindling needed to be split for a start, so I left that for my son to organise and stretched out on one of the bunks and fell asleep. I slept much longer than I intended and when I woke the fire was blazing and it was dark. Obviously my body was still adjusting to having sat upright for all those hours on those cramped and narrow seats over the Pacific. Talking to my grandson for the first time, although marvellous, was also perhaps a stressful experience.

In one corner of the main part of the cabin there was a shelf where people had left books, magazines and games. Ned and Matthew were playing chess. Dinner simply required heating on the top of the stove and we passed the evening telling stories instead of watching bad television. It was very enjoyable, and we all agreed that people should stay in log cabins more often.

We told lots of stories. I told Ned about climbing mountains in Greenland and how back in 1957 with some other geologists I had measured the size of the Atlantic Ocean and proved it was nineteen centimetres wider than when Alfred Wegener first measured it in 1930. That, I told Ned, was just before he fell into a nearby crevasse and disappeared forever. Ned was impressed, not because continents moved, but because they moved so slowly. He didn't know anything about glaciers and crevasses so I had to explain. I livened things up by telling him how a musk ox chased my friend John Soulsby up a hill and I captured it all on a movie camera. That film, I told him, was somewhere in his basement and if his dad got it reprocessed onto a DVD he could watch the whole thing on his computer or TV.

Eventually we went to bed. Ned climbed his ladder to his top bunk. On his way, he said, 'Grandpa, the best thing about staying in a log cabin is the stories.'

His father took a bedroom downstairs to the left and I just pulled up my sleeping bag and slept on the couch in front of the fire. From time to time during the night I threw on another couple of logs.

As I lay there in front of the fire it seemed to me there were five things a person could do every day to be healthy, hopeful and happy and I wanted to pass these on to my grandson. I knew I couldn't just tell him; I had to demonstrate by my example. The first is to develop friendships so I always smile and greet people politely giving them a chance to speak if they want to. Being physically active is always important, although I don't have a high opinion of organised games. Thirdly, everyone every day until the day they die should foster curiosity about the world. Doing this achieves the fourth and most important thing, which is continuing your education throughout your life. The last is not to think about money all the time. Instead offer help and services to all. These five things maintain good mental health.

10

The Mad Swede

By now it was Thursday morning. Ned and I went down to the river and between the little fellow's questions, each of which I answered immediately, I found myself thinking about the other rivers that flowed to the west instead of east like the Cowichan. Ned, I think, became conscious of his grandfather's meditative mood and experimented for himself lowering his fly into a small patch of slightly less fierce water that was protected by a huge rock. It was an excellent place for a steelhead to lie, but in these conditions there was no response. At this time of the year because of the spring melt the fishing in rivers everywhere on the island was particularly bad.

I thought again about the one occasion I had fished the Nitinat with Big Arthur and a friend he had brought along. Mostly I fished that river that ran into Nitinat Lake alone, but Arthur's friend had apparently always lacked success as a fisherman and Arthur, although he hadn't said so, had decided to bring this stranger along and give him to me for instruction.

When we got to the river Arthur shot off a kilometre upstream, where he knew a good place to fish, and he left me at a less desirable spot to help the beginner. Teaching is a never-ending learning process for anyone who attempts it. But it is a valuable experience because, as time goes on, the teacher learns that there are very few correct answers.

On that far-off day in the sixties I stood at the end of a gravel bar with the person I have thought of ever since as the mad Swede. I don't actually know if Erik was a Swede, but he wore a white peaked sailor's cap like I remember Swedish students wearing in Europe. Arthur told me his friend could never catch fish, and years later I realised it was the white cap that was the problem. A flash of white high above the water looks like the white underside of the wings of a predatory bird. Fish instinctively dash for cover.

So Erik and I were left on the tip of a stretch of gravel sticking out into the river casting to a couple of steelhead that I had spotted some way upstream. Erik stood meekly by and asked me to demonstrate how it was done. It was a very long cast so I had to double-haul, a difficult operation which puts quite a powerful bend in the rod. About thirty metres away my fly hit the water. I then allowed it to sink, and bumped it a few times past the first steelhead and finally irritated it into striking. It was such a long cast that the fish could not see us. I led that steelhead away from the other fish. It ran out into the big pool and I fought it hard. Finally, I drew the fish in and killed it by whacking it on the head. I laid it on the gravel bar behind us and that was it for my day.

'Your turn now,' I said to Erik, but he made some excuse, saying that he hadn't really understood what was happening, so would I do everything again and hook another fish. Then, he said, he would play it and reel it in. I thought this a silly idea and refused, but eventually I agreed to do it because he could not possibly cast to where the other fish was lying. I made a second cast and the second steelhead was now on. It was bigger and harder to land than the first.

The fish was leaping all over the river when I heard the most terrible noise behind me. Erik was swearing in a mixture of Swedish and English, and I twisted my body, still fighting the steelhead, to see an angry adult black bear. It was standing up and roaring while Erik hurled grapefruit-sized rocks at its head with deadly accuracy. The bear didn't like it at all.

'He's trying to get your fish,' shouted Erik.

'Let him have it,' I shouted back.

'Not bloody likely,' shouted Erik and he hit the bear with another rock squarely between the eyes.

It was quite ridiculous: a three-hundred-kilogram male black bear being attacked by an angry, bilingual, swearing seventy-kilogram Swede wearing a ridiculous white yachting cap. I suppose the contest didn't really last that long, but in the end the bear retreated into the bush very annoyed. It started ripping out small trees and throwing them into the river. I landed the second steelhead about the same time and Erik and I avoided the angry bear on the left bank by wading and half swimming across the river and upstream to join Big Arthur.

When we got there Erik gave me the smaller fish. 'How did you do?' Big Arthur asked and Erik showed him the larger fish and said, 'This is mine.'

I learned quite a lot from that day. Some people can be more aggressive than bears and sometimes outwit them, but I still think it is largely luck—you can't rely on it. I learned that some people are possessive about fish, even more so than bears are. Also, for some people size does matter especially with fish and it is important to have the biggest one. I still think Erik should have allowed that hungry bear to have the steelhead.

Since that day I have had lots of encounters with grizzlies as well as black bears. Of the two I think black bears are probably more dangerous simply because they are not monarch of all they survey and are forced to use subterfuge. Most of the time neither of these bears are much of a problem and when I look at the world around me, read a newspaper or watch television, there is no doubt in my mind that man is the world's most dangerous animal.

I talked to Ned about this and he agreed it would have been more sensible to have left the bear with the first fish and have gone fishing somewhere else.

'Do you think we might meet a bear today, Grandpa?' he asked. I reassured him that if we did we would quietly move away and if we didn't have any fish the bear probably wouldn't bother us.

I told Ned I loved the area around Nitinat Lake, even though the wind that funnelled down the lake in the afternoons made it much more dangerous to canoe than the slightly larger Cowichan Lake. I had spent a lot of time there fishing the rivers that entered it and exploring the numerous other lakes in the area that nearly all connected up. It seems now, looking back to those days in the late sixties when I lived in Meade's cabin on the North Arm, that every time I went out with my rod I caught fish.

One day I had a visitor from Australia: the museum

curator in the geology department at the Australian National University. I had known George Halford well when I was teaching at the ANU and we had fished together on several occasions when collecting rock and fossil specimens. The most memorable was at the beautiful Blue Waterhole in the Snowy Mountains where I was introducing George, a skilled bait fisher, to the joys of the artificial fly. The limit for trout in those days in Australia was ten fish. I have never liked the idea of limits because many anglers will continue to fish until they catch the limit as George was trying to do that day. But after landing six rainbow trout he hooked himself in the back of the head and I had to remove the fly from his skull with a pair of pliers in the headlights of the Jeep.

I took George fishing in the big pool in the Cowichan River just below the bridge. If I remember correctly he wanted to fish in the river because it had just been listed as one of the top six rivers in the world in *Field & Stream*. I suppose George fished for about two hours and I paddled the canoe around the big pool. We saw the odd swirl of what looked like a fish, but George didn't have any luck. Finally, he suggested I try. I was reluctant because I really wanted him to connect, but he insisted. I think maybe it was on the second or third cast that I had a fish on. It jumped all over the big pool and towed the canoe around until George got it into the boat. It was beautiful and silver and I showed

George the fresh sea lice on its body. Sea lice can only live for about twelve hours in fresh water so the fish must have entered the river that day from the sea. I think it weighed about five kilograms. George was as thrilled as if he had landed it himself. We took it back to the cabin and made dinner.

Until that time I had never really fished the Cowichan. I had always fished to the west because the country there was deserted and wild. The fish I caught with George was the first I ever caught in the river, but was not the last. Later in my time in the cabin I fished the river occasionally with a much older man, Professor Lewis Clark, who was writing a book on the botany of the region and used to come to the Cowichan to fish. I learned a lot from watching that old man who was an effortless caster and a skilful angler. Like me he didn't care about the size or weight of a fish, he fished because he loved the river. Much of the time he just photographed flowers for his book.

About this time my new rod arrived from Scotland. In the sixties quality rods were made of split cane and the cane was always Tonkin bamboo. The normal fly rod in those days was only eight feet (2.4 metres) long in order to keep it as light as possible but this special rod, made for me by Rob Wilson of Brora, was eight foot, nine inches (2.7 metres). It was intended to replace the big salmon rod that had snapped in two when I was fishing the river below the Chief's Hole. It was stiffer than my regular trout rod as well as eight centimetres longer but still very light. Rob built it especially for me and modelled it on what was then the world's most famous distance-casting rod, the Kohinoor made by Hardy, and he only charged me six pounds.

Many fly rods even today are still about this length for it is argued that continual casting demands a light rod. True, most of the rivers I fished to the west of the lake did not require much long casting, but it seemed to me then that the Cowichan, which was a big river and fished more often than the western rivers, might require a more sophisticated rod capable of casting further than was normal.

I realise now that all young anglers think long casting is necessary. It is a big mistake. Armed with this equipment and a stripping basket to hold the loose line I could cast a shooting head right across the river, but I would have been far better off watching Lewis Clark who always seemed to catch fish right in front of his feet. Why I thought I needed this extra tackle I don't really know because most of the steelhead I had caught so far I had landed using my lighter trout rod.

The new rod of course was designed to be used for salmon as well as large steelhead, but now, forty years later, I think it was not really needed. The eleven-foot (3.3-metre) rod I use now is perhaps not quite as light as the old standard nine footer popular in the sixties but it fishes much better. Every foot added to a rod doubles its usefulness but for rods longer than eleven feet one is probably forced to cast using both hands.

The fish I landed in the river pool with George that in our excitement we identified as a fresh run silver salmon I now think was a lone steelhead. We just assumed it was a salmon because of its size. Most people at that time believed that steelhead were trout and even biologists had not yet worked out they are in fact the ancestors of the five other Pacific salmon—the chinook or spring, the coho or silver, the sockeye, the pink or humpback and the chum or dog. There were so many large fish in those days that people paid less attention to them and knew far less about them than they do today.

The big fish we caught hadn't been in the river long enough for even the faintest rainbow stripe to develop on its flanks, for as I said it had only been a few hours since it had left the sea. I think now the fish was one of that special race of steelhead that went right up through the lake to spawn at the far end of Shaw Creek on the north-west side of Cowichan Lake. When it reached that lovely creek, much beloved by Farson, it would develop the characteristic rainbow stripe and be ready to breed.

Back in the sixties, I was beginning to notice subtle differences in the populations of the different rivers but I had a long way to go. The natural state of affairs was that the steelhead that ran up the river I called the Lost River to the west were different from the steelhead that ran up the Cowichan, and in the Cowichan there were probably two races: one that spawned in that river and perhaps other races that spawned in the rivers that ran into the lake. In every river I fished I noticed slight variations. I knew that what I was thinking was not proven science, but it was certainly a possibility.

The steelhead, nowadays properly recognised as a salmon, differed from the other species on the Pacific coast in several ways. In the ocean the fish was unique because it mostly swam alone, not in shoals; it travelled further than any other salmon and returned to the river every month of the year in relatively small numbers, instead of at a set time. But, most important, unlike the other Pacific salmon, it does not die on spawning. Anglers recognised that in all rivers there were two types: the smaller summer steelhead and the much larger winter steelhead. Summer fish fed actively in the rivers and were more fun to fish. Winter runs were more inclined to take bait and were harder to tempt with a fly. Both were very strong, athletic fish and it was very exciting to get one on.

In the Old World there were salmon and trout and if we were lucky we also discovered char. In the New World of America, especially as one travelled further west, there were many more species and I wondered why the west was so well endowed. Living in Meade's cabin I had plenty of time to think about it. I knew that some similar species of animals were capable of interbreeding but the offspring were sterile. I wasn't sure if this also applied to fish. Two very similar looking species of trout are the rainbow and the cutthroat, but they behave very differently and are always found in different parts of the river. In the sixties most cutthroat were small and they were regarded as inferior fish. They were very easy to catch then and every kid caught hundreds of them. Adults considered them unfit to eat and used them as fertiliser. The big cutthroat I caught at the mouth of the Robertson seemed somehow different, and I think that perhaps it was.

In nature, when rainbow trout and cutthroat confront each other they become aggressive. The cutthroat flares his gills, faces the other fish and displays the great red gash across his throat. The rainbow turns sideways and displays the red stripe along its lateral line, and the cutthroat then meekly goes away. To my eye the cutthroat looks much fiercer but the sheer nonchalance of the rainbow seems to be more effective. Cutthroat are nearly always relegated to a shallower part of the river with the result that, for the smaller cutthroat at least, they are easier to catch. At least that is the way it used to be; cutthroat were mainly caught by small boys and they usually finished up dumped on the garden.

Forty years later, we know better thanks to Robert Behnke of Colorado State University. Because of his work we now recognise fourteen subspecies of cutthroat trout, and he tells us that in the waters of America they are like the canary in the coal mine. These now-rare fish have been forced to become more selective in their habitat, and much harder to catch than they once were. This vanishing native deserves our respect. The big one I caught in Bear Lake nearly half a century ago with the help of Big Arthur certainly fought far better than any hatchery-bred rainbow.

If we look at the family trees of trout and salmon it looks as if the circum-arctic chars and the Eurasian huchen are the most primitive forms. Later the closely related Atlantic salmon and brown trout developed; then came the different kinds of cutthroat trout and, finally, the rainbow trout. This latter species is genetically almost identical to the steelhead from which the five other species of Pacific salmon developed. This picture makes sense to me and has probably by now been confirmed by studies of the fishes' DNA. But for the practical angler there are lots of other mysteries still to be revealed, for fish of the same species from different river systems often differ quite a lot.

When I first started fishing near Meade's cabin, it seemed that the fish from each of the local rivers were slightly different: the giant coho in the river I called the Chief and the long, lean athletic steelhead in the Lost. The steelhead that I had caught in the Cowichan was plumper and I took it for a salmon. I suppose I was beginning to recognise that each river had its own unique population of fish. I hesitate to use words like race or nationality but steelhead in the Lost River were excitable and friendly in the way I remember Italians, and the steelhead in the Cowichan were more distant and reserved like the English. Their characters were just a little different but whether it was due to their environment or genetics I was unable to decide. Nevertheless, after a while I could just look at a fish and make a fairly good guess about its provenance.

Perhaps the biggest problem with rivers today is the arrogant way we humans have been restocking them and tampering with the genetic make-up of the fish. We seem to be convinced we can do better than nature. Rivers are far better off if they are left alone.

Nevertheless it is now commonplace for truckloads of hatchery-bred fish to be dumped into lakes and rivers all over the world and the kind of fish dumped are genetically engineered in the same way as our farm animals have been through selective breeding. The best fish are always those that are wild. Hatchery trout are not worth catching and are never as good as the original.

Frayed fins are a sign of overcrowding and are never seen in wild fish. When fish are fed pellets in crowded tanks their fins get damaged in the rush for food. This feeding procedure makes the trout much more likely to take a splashy cast which would put a wild fish down. Here's a tip for anyone buying trout or salmon in a fish shop: look at the tail fin. It will show wear if the fish has been in a crowded tank. Then remember, the food we give to farm fish is in the form of pellets full of antibiotics, growth hormones and colouring matter to make the fish's flesh red. You are far better off catching your own if you can find a place where the trout are still wild.

We need to interfere less with nature and leave our rivers to lie fallow the way farmers used to leave fields alone for a while to allow them to regain fertility. If we closed all rivers to fishing for a few years on a cyclical basis the fish would probably eventually recover and there would be no need for restocking.

I was thinking about all these things and had lost track of time. Then Ned came up to ask me if we could explore downstream. Our foray travelling up the river had been unsuccessful, but I could tell he had gained something from it.

'There will probably be even more fast water down there, Grandpa,' he said, 'but let's go and look anyway just in case.'

'Good idea,' I said.

We crossed the footbridge which led to the old logging road, and then Ned and I followed a rough trail that veered to the right. There were lots of rushes in the area and a bit of a swamp, and it was quite hard going for a while until we reached the river. There appeared to be a narrow channel separating a rocky tree-covered islet. The main part of the river flowed on the other side of the islet. The water in the narrow channel was also very fast and it was clear that it had overflowed into the swamp. It didn't seem to be suitable water to hold fish.

'You know what, Ned,' I said. 'I think we are skunked.'

'Skunked? Grandpa, what does that mean?'

'It's what Canadian anglers say when they are not getting any fish. It's the nearest we get to swearing.'

'What do they say in other countries, Grandpa?'

'They are more polite and they just say they had a blank day.'

We then wended our way back through the swamp and along the trail to the cabin. Ned's dad had just made some tea.

'How did you do?' Matthew asked.

'We had a blank day,' said Ned.

11

Teaching a Boy to Fish

The secret of teaching has always been not to let it be too obvious. I was fortunate because I had some of the best teachers in the world. Most of these were academics who came straight from universities and, luckily, had never been trained to teach. Instead they mumbled to themselves, grunted and were absent-minded, but they were generous people who knew their subjects better than anyone else and they patiently answered questions. I wanted to be like them.

Today it has become possible for people with no real knowledge of a subject to teach it. Administrators like this idea because it is more flexible, but having teachers desperately trying to stay ahead of the brighter students is not the way to go. It is no wonder that under this more modern system students are learning a lot less.

When I was a boy in a single-sex school the teachers I admired the most were all enthusiasts for their subject and I learned my lessons because I wanted to not because I was being told I had to. My teachers never seemed to care about anything much, but it was clear they loved their subject and they passed the information on without any obvious effort. In short they never tried to force anything into my brain, instead by their actions they drew things out that were already partly inside. They polished these ideas with discussion and made them shine. Every young brain is full of thoughtful but often slightly crazy ideas and needs constant reassurance.

Lastly, it is important to recognise that there is a difference between the sexes. Boys need to like and admire their teachers. Girls, on the other hand, have the ability to learn in spite of teachers. This is probably why nowadays with much poorer teachers girls are pulling ahead of boys. In a perfect world every person would have the right kind of teaching.

With these thoughts in mind I decided never to show Ned how to do anything unless he asked. As the days passed on the river I would sit down on a log and start fiddling with my tackle and notice that he often watched what I was doing out of the corner of his eye. I would say, as if talking to myself when tying a blood knot, 'Four and a half turns then though the loop.' One day he asked me why I did only four and a half turns and I told him that it was the minimum number and I couldn't count any more because it was too boring.

He laughed. 'Can I do five?' he said.

I told him that was a good idea because three or four turns probably weren't quite enough and six or seven didn't make the knot any better and were a waste of time. The effect of this was that Ned would never forget the four-and-a-half-turn blood knot.

'Why is it called the blood knot, Grandpa?'

I told him it was invented by surgeons when they were doing operations like removing an appendix. It had to be a good knot, I said, because they didn't want to have to cut someone open again because the knot came undone. Ned asked if knowing the blood knot would make him a doctor and I told him he would have to catch a fish first and learn how to gut it properly.

'Medicine is a bit like fishing,' I said. 'There is a lot to learn and it takes a lot of time.'

As often happens when teaching someone else how to do a thing the teacher learns something too. I threaded the line through the eye of the hook to tie the blood knot under the watchful eye of my grandson and I started to wonder how Juliana Berners fixed her imitation stonefly to the horsehair line. I remembered that she specified the hair had to come from the tail of a stallion because a mare's tail hair was weaker, but she said nothing about tying on the hook.

Then I remembered the eye didn't appear on hooks until probably late in the nineteenth century, so the abbess, our 'Father' Walton and the wonderful Russian writer Sergei Timofeevich Aksakov all tied their hooks to the line some other way. My mind went back to Aksakov's classic *Notes on Fishing* and its epigraph: 'I venture into nature's world, the world of serenity and freedom.' I wondered how those words got past the strict Russian censorship in 1847.

Sitting on this log by the Cowichan River in May 2008 I tried to recall Aksakov's chapter on the hook. I remembered it began by saying, 'The best hooks are English ones,' which is still true today, followed by several pages on how to choose a good one. Then my memory kicked in again and I recalled he said something about the ends of hooks in those days having a shank with a little nub at the top whose 'shoulders must be wide and not sharp', so obviously the hook didn't have an eye until after he wrote this. Fishers then must have used a different kind of knot and I would have to try to work out what it was. My small grandson had got my brain working. We were each good for the other.

'What are you thinking about, Grandpa?' Ned asked.

I told him a bit about Aksakov going fishing in Russia and that he was a great writer. The next best thing to fishing I said was reading about it, and reading was marvellous because there were so many great books. Then, the knot having been tied and questions answered, I got up from my log and we went further up the river.

The bush was thick and the trail meandered a lot so it was extremely difficult to get near enough to the water to fish. Young Ned's tackle irritated me because it was too short, but the boy persisted and that was the most important thing. His rod was only a metre long and the reel was a cheap fixed-spool reel with a very light nylon line. True it was easier for him to cast with this American-style rod, but it was too short to poke through the bushes and reach the places close to the bank where, in conditions like these, a fish might choose to lie.

The emphasis is all on casting nowadays and nearly all anglers stand right at the edge of the river or, worse, enter the water in order to cast. In some rivers wading is necessary to present the fly correctly but the angler is usually better off avoiding it.

I decided that I would have to make sure to buy Ned a longer rod fitted with a more appropriate reel at a later date, after he had caught his first fish. It would have made a lot more sense to do it immediately but the last thing I wanted to do was criticise Matthew's choice of tackle. Instead I tried to set an example by trying to poke my three-metre rod through the bush then muttering that it was a bit too short. Ned and I never talked about it but I could tell that he realised he would have been better off with more rod.

At one stage he did complain that both our rods were too short and I told him how, when I was his age, I lived very near the famous River Lea where Izaak Walton did most of his fishing. I told him it was much slower than the Cowichan but about as wide, and when I was a boy many anglers didn't have reels and used rods that were about twelve metres long. They tied their lines to the end of the rod and removed sections of the rod from the butt to bring the fish in.

'Didn't anyone have reels in those days, Grandpa?'

'Some rich people did but most of us couldn't afford them.' I told Ned about my first rod, which had no rings so it couldn't be used with a reel. It was called a 'boy's rod' and was made out of bamboo. It was five and a half metres long and broke down into about six pieces. It cost me two shillings, about a penny a foot, and I bought it at the nearby Avenue Cycle Store. I was digging potatoes on Edward's Farm at the time because all the men were away fighting the war and for this hard work I earned five pence an hour so I had to work for nearly a day to get the money to pay for it. I tied five metres of cheap cotton line to the end and fished with that. I used to lash a cotton bag with the rod inside it to the crossbar of my bike and ride to the river with a tin of maggots in my pocket to catch perch and roach for there hadn't been any trout or salmon in the Lea for hundreds of years.

Ned was curious about the different kinds of fish that we could find in this Canadian river and I told him that there were two kinds. There were the resident fish who spent their whole lives in one small part of the river like the pool we were looking at, and they were trout. And there were the visitors that came in every year from the sea in order to spawn, and they were salmon. I also explained to him that there were half a dozen different kinds of salmon but the biggest of all came in when the current was strongest like it was at this moment and that was in the spring.

'Maybe I could get one of those salmon,' he said.

I explained they were as long as his rod and at least twice as heavy as he was and they would pull him in. 'Besides,' I said, 'the best ones to eat are the ones that fit into the frying pan and just fill a plate.'

He thought about this for a moment. 'If we catch a big one we can cut it up and put it into tins.'

I told him how years ago, in the year men landed on

the moon, I had been at Campbell River and thought the same thing and tinned a lot of big salmon myself.

'What was it like, Grandpa?'

'Not as good as a smaller fish straight out of the river.'

We continued our way upstream looking for a place to fish, but everywhere the river was too fast to sink a fly and, even if we'd had any worms, we didn't have enough lead to get one down into the kind of places where the trout would be hiding. In the end, after a walk where we mainly just looked at the water, we gave up. Probably most fishing is like this: you go for a walk along a river. But books, and especially magazines, don't tell the reader about the blank days; instead they are full of pictures of trophy fish and triumphant anglers.

Amazingly, young Ned understood the importance of this quest. When we reached the cabin he turned to me and said, 'You know, Grandpa, when we do get a fish, because we know how hard it is, it will be even more exciting.'

I smiled 'You are right. I think you are a fisherman already.' This was true education, I thought to myself.

Often when we were staying in the cabin or walking along the river we told stories. They came from both of us, but Ned asked so many questions that many of the stories were mine. That is the chief purpose of the old: to tell stories and to keep them as close to the truth as possible. Some of the characters in these stories came to life for Ned and he began to ask me questions like, 'What would Big Arthur do here?' or to say, 'If we see a cougar we had better call Donny Palmer.'

Gradually, perhaps because of my bias towards steelhead, he asked more and more about this magnificent fish. I told him about places like the Lost River where Big Arthur once took nineteen fish and how on the way to Steelhead Rock he would run seven metres across the slippery log over the deep canyon of Wolf Creek in his caulked boots and laugh at me slipping around on the log in my rubber-soled climbing boots.

I told my grandson about the huge Douglas fir forest above the canyon. The trees were giants and were so big no light came through. The forest had a completely bare floor covered with nothing except a carpet of millions and millions of flat, sharp-pointed needles a couple of centimetres long. But now sadly the great firs have gone and the forest that had been above that river for more than ten thousand years has been replaced by the small fast-growing *Pinus radiata* plantation trees from California. It is the classic fairytale of the Aladdin swindle when the wicked peddler gets the magic lamp from the poor ignorant boy by offering him new wares for old. I thought about fairytales and wondered if Ned knew this one, but I didn't ask him—it was too sad even thinking about the loss of those giant Douglas firs.

We were now most of the way through our week in the cabin and all we had managed to do so far was look at the water. Fishing can be like this. What one is really doing is exploring, learning about a place and hoping to find a good place to fish. In Australia it is the same except the emphasis is different; there the first thing one has to do is *find* some water. The greatest rivers in Australia, the Snowy and the Murray, are often barely flowing so one is forced to go higher and higher into the mountains and then, even after walking a long way, the tiny creeks are often also dry. Fishing in fresh water in Australia takes a long time. Here in Canada, during the spring at least, there was too much water and it was pretty obvious the Cowichan could not be fished for at least another week.

Few Australian rivers are youthful; a river as young as the Cowichan possibly does not exist there. Australian rivers wander slowly, eventually leaving cut-offs that poets call billabongs and geologists refer to as oxbow lakes. In dry periods these rivers dry up completely as the water-table drops and all the water seeps underground. Rivers I had fished in the fifties in Australia, the Snowy River being the obvious example, had lost so much water that the land around them had almost died. It was hard to imagine something similar happening to the Cowichan; it was a rough, bare-knuckled and brawling stream. Yet because of the development I had seen and the small number of salmon in the run, I sensed the river's days were numbered.

I was the first to wake the next day and so as not to disturb Ned and Matthew I walked down to the river for one more look just in case it had calmed. The snow on the nearby mountains was disappearing fast but the river was just as high. So I decided the best thing for us to do that day would be to fish the westward-flowing Robertson River. I had told Ned about the cougar I had seen crossing the old logging bridge all those years ago. It was quite shallow there, a good place for cutthroat trout. Not far below it was Bear Lake where I had caught my record cutthroat. I walked back to the cabin where the fire was out and the stay-in-beds were just getting up.

It is easy to fritter time away in a log cabin deep in the woods so, feeling rather like a tour guide, I made an announcement. 'Today we are going into Lake Cowichan for breakfast, then we will go to the tackle shop to see if there is anything we need and then we will fish the Robertson River.' I waited while they washed the sleep out of their eyes, and we walked down the trail to the car.

We ate breakfast at the Riverside Inn and the food was excellent: eggs done anyway you wanted, bacon and pancakes with lots of real maple syrup, much better than the 'maple flavoured' stuff you often get in Australia. They kept bringing pancakes until we were full and I noticed young Ned ate more pancakes than his father and probably three or four times as many as I did. He also drank lots of orange juice while his father and I got stuck into the bottomless cups of good Colombian coffee you get when you have breakfast in Canada. Awake and alert, everyone was ready to fish so we walked across the town bridge and looked at the river. We saw the odd sign of the few salmon occasionally rolling near the surface. Then we entered the main street.

The town had changed quite a bit in forty years and there were a lot more shops. The old tackle shop was not there, but on the left-hand side of the road going towards Bear Lake we found a new one and went inside. Tackle shops are founts of information about the state of the rivers in the region, and most anglers usually need some simple things like a couple of new leaders or a few extra hooks. In return the owner is always happy to show the angler the latest reels, rods and other more expensive pieces of tackle and the customer often ends up making a purchase.

I was pleased to see that this excellent store sold natural bait and had some really good free-running centre-pin reels. With the tremendous increase in fly-fishing these days modern anglers seem to hamper themselves by using heavier reels with a permanent click, often a large arbour and an adjustable drag. They are deluded; the older type of centre-pins are much more versatile because they can be used in many different ways: with the check on when fly fishing for trout, and with the check off when free lining for salmon or 'long trotting' for coarser fish. You only need to buy a single reel. In most places simple on-off regulators on reels seem to be disappearing, but this store had some of the best reels I had seen for years. Lake Cowichan anglers had not abandoned them for fixed-spool reels or special fly-reels like anglers everywhere else. Perhaps there were some experts like Big Arthur still around.

Juliana Berners and Izaak Walton did not use line-storing devices at all—when a fish was too big to land right away they were forced to throw their rod into the river and hope to retrieve it later when the fish was worn out from towing it around.

Since then, anglers have learned it's a good idea to store a bit of extra line in places where the fish are big and strong, and the more knowledgeable ones know the simple winch is the most practical way of doing it. Unfortunately most modern anglers seem to believe fishing is mainly about casting further than anyone else and so they tend to use shorter, stiffer rods and environmentally hazardous mono-filament line cast from mechanically complicated fixed-spool reels. This line, a petroleum by-product, casts so easily, but it 'remembers' it has been tightly coiled and consequently often forms huge tangles. Because it is so cheap it then gets thrown away. Usually it ends up in the river where it traps the feet of birds and generally threatens wildlife for years. Many nature lovers as well as an increasing number of anglers think that this dangerous and nearly invisible line should be banned.

Wandering around the tackle shop in Lake Cowichan I found a glass cabinet full of second-hand fishing tackle and the first thing I noticed was an old polished leather leader wallet about twelve centimetres square that looked very much like the one I had bought in Scotland and lost when I lived in Meade's cabin all those years ago.

Inside it there were the usual felt drying pads and three parchment pockets with a small collection of what Americans call leaders and the British call casts. They are short pieces of cat-gut that anglers formerly used between the end of their thicker fishing line and the hook. They were still in their envelopes. One was from the great company of Allcock's who made the Aerial—the world's best reel—and the Wallis Wizard rod. The red leader envelope still had the price sixpence halfpenny written on it neatly in ink. Of course I had to have this old wallet for it was exactly the same as the one I had lost. Now that I have had it a while I have convinced myself it is the same one. The price was only twenty dollars so I paid the man and now we had an excuse for examining all his gear.

I bought a few other fishing 'necessities' including a bone-handled knife for my grandson. The knife was twelve centimetres long when folded, weighed about a hundred and fifty grams and had a large single blade. It was deliberately too big and heavy to carry in a pocket and was to be kept in his pack. A knife was, I told him, man's most important tool and must never be abused. It was great to see Ned's face: he knew then he was being treated like a grown-up and was now a real fisherman.

Next I had a yarn with the owner, Gordy. Like all tackle-shop proprietors he was an interesting and knowledgeable guy. Just as we were leaving the store he wished us good fishing and showed me a small jar of orange paste. He told me that when moulded around the hook it was the best bait ever invented and was used by all the local fishermen. I laughed and said I was familiar with its magic, as forty years ago I used to fish with the guy that probably invented the stuff. I told him about Big Arthur. He was amazed and said that his supplier was the same man. 'Would you like to see him again?'

'Of course,' I said. But when he tried telephoning there was no answer, and when he rang Arthur's son it turned out that Big Arthur was away for a few days and would not be back until the day after I flew back to Australia. I would have loved to have seen the old rogue and I thought about what might have happened if we could have fished together once again.

As I left, Gordy gave me his card and later when I looked at it more closely I noticed his last name was March. Was he descended from Henry March, the first settler on the lake who built his place at Honeymoon Bay out of hemlock logs? I made a mental note to speak to the tackle dealer about his ancestor when I returned to the store.

We then drove to the Robertson River. It was always a much more ordinary and friendly river than the Cowichan. Negley Farson called it the Robinson. I know he fished it quite often so he should have got the name right, but he was a bit like Humpty Dumpty and was both imperious as well as careless with names. All these years later it was no surprise to me that he eventually fell off his wall.

Since I last saw the Robertson the geography of the river had changed. There was a new road bridge and I think it was in a slightly different place so it took quite a time to find the old logging railway line. All the rails and cross-ties had been pulled up, and when we reached the place where the railroad crossed the river we found the old trestle also was gone. However the log posts that supported the bridge were still in the river, and at the base of the nearest one on our side there were a few rocks and a small patch of weed. The water was absolutely clear, and I could see the nose of quite a large trout just sticking out from this excellent feeding position. The gravel bar I had fished from all those years ago had shifted to the other side of the river and without the trestle we could not get to it. And at the bottom of this clear, apparently slow-moving stream, there was now a lot more sand.

Well out of sight of the fish we had a council of war. As far as we could see there was only one fish in the river and we had to decide if we should fish at all. I was fairly certain that there were probably quite a few cutthroat in Bear Lake lower down but, because there was only one fish in sight, we faced an ethical question, and I thought it was great for Ned that we had a serious discussion first.

Although I had spotted the fish I was not interested in fishing for it because I wanted my grandson to catch a fish, but my son decided he was probably the only one who could cast that far. So the boy fished the edge higher up dapping his fly wherever there was a possible lie for a trout under a rocky part of the bank, and the man tried to get his line down deep enough for the fly to interest the fish.

Neither was successful because the flow, although it didn't look it, was too fast. The intermediate line that Matthew was using (always the best plastic line to use) couldn't get down to the fish so this nice cutthroat lived to fight another day. If there had been a good lie where the boy was dapping he might have found something, so along the bank there were probably no other fish.

Eventually we gave up for the day, but a valuable lesson had been learned. To reach a fish in a position like that in that kind of flow, the angler needs to be further away. If it had been possible to reach the end of the gravel bar from which I had fished forty years earlier, then by free lining instead of casting that fish could have ended up in our frying pan. We had an interesting discussion about conservation and in the end we decided that if we had managed to hook and land this fish we would have let it go.

12

Mistakes

Learning is about recognising mistakes and then being able
to remind yourself when faced with a similar situation of
your former stupidity. During my walks along the river and
talks with Ned I told him that I had made a lot of mistakes
and that sometimes I thought I must have had something
lacking, a screw loose as we used to say at school. I would tell
him these things whenever he felt he had done something
silly, and I tried to explain that even grandfathers feel stupid
sometimes and slightly out of phase.

I said that in the late sixties, when I had been living in
Meade's cabin for nearly two years, I felt more lost than ever.
I was becoming like a lonely long-distance runner, which

is what I most enjoyed when at school. We had physical training every day (now called physical education because it sounds better) and games twice a week, but there were only three compulsory activities. They were cross-country running, boxing and chess. Every boy had to participate in these three activities but in everything else there was a choice—if cricket bored you, you could play tennis or run. In winter, you could play rugby or soccer or run. I preferred to run.

Thankfully, my school did not glorify team sports, it accepted the herd instinct in boys but felt it more important that we became individuals. It believed in self-reliance more than anything else and encouraged us to be ourselves. It was probably this kind of training, where teachers trusted their charges, that enabled me to become a solo mountaineer and eventually to sail north alone in my boat.

I told my grandson that I thought regimentation had never been a good idea because it encouraged individuals to be too dependent on others. Doing things alone forced one to think in order to survive. So, I said to Ned, whenever I went out into the great forest in western Canada in the past, which was every day, I learned something new and this was the important thing.

My problem, I said, was not in absorbing new information, it was in putting the pieces together so that they made sense. I was trying to solve a geological puzzle, where many of the pieces were living things. I knew I was in a position to turn the key but I couldn't find the lock, or perhaps it was the other way round—I was not seeing something so big and so basic it was like failing to notice your own nose. I talked to Ned about noses when I described to him how I wandered aimlessly through these woods as a young man, and we laughed a lot because we decided everybody could see their own nose quite well but ignored it as mostly it was convenient to do so.

Ned proved how silly it was to keep noticing his own nose by bumping into a small tree. We concluded clowns had red noses like stop lights so they wouldn't keep bumping into things. The odd thing was they bumped into more things than ordinary people did so, we wondered, what use was a red nose?

'Maybe,' said Ned, 'they use it to attract fish.' He had a good sense of humour. I told him that red was the first colour to disappear at depth. I said that probably accounted for the success of the metal Daredevil spoon which had a thin sliver of white in the middle with the rest of the spoon blood-red. It put out a lot of vibration and attracted the fish, and they hit it hard because in deeper water they only saw the white part and thought it was the right size to eat.

We had elected to fish only with home-tied flies, but

we agreed we would use bait perhaps towards the end of the trip if we got really desperate. We didn't even consider the commonest modern way to fish which is to use weighted plastic metal or lures like the Daredevil spoon. With them we might have been able to get closer to the bottom of this wild river. Lures are much more expensive than flies and get lost and snagged much more easily because they have several sets of triple hooks. Also, to use lures we would have to carry a heavy tackle box and specialised rods and reels. I wanted Ned to learn the old way first.

Every month in this wild country there was something different to see and I tried to make it clear to Ned that it was not always what one expected and often differed from the common opinion. I now knew he was pretty sensible so I told him the story about Erik and the bear for it was clear he would not do anything foolish. And, I said to him, who would have thought that I would witness an unarmed man stupid enough to attack and drive off a bear? Why did the wolverine just snarl and not attack me, and why hadn't I shot it even though I had a gun? Why was it that after perhaps a hundred casts George had hooked nothing, then after only two or three tries I got the fish of the day? I had hundreds of questions like these and didn't have any of the answers. Why, if cougars were so dangerous and there were so many of them, weren't more people attacked? Why do fish eat worms? The two of us, the old man and the boy, discussed all the possibilities as we walked from one fishing place to another along this wild, roaring river.

I told Ned that when I finally left Meade's cabin I was having all sorts of doubts because I felt I was no closer to solving the mystery of the great batholith. I used long words like this when talking to him, and when he asked I explained that this fairly modern word came from two older ones: *bathos* which meant deep-seated and *lithos* which meant stone. We picked up a piece of the batholith, a granite rock lying on the trail, and I showed him the minerals it contained: the hard, acid quartz, which broke down into sand, and some feldspar and mica, which broke down into clay. I then said we were standing on the largest body of granite in the world. It was the world's most infertile and inhospitable rock, yet we were surrounded by a mass of life greater than anywhere else.

I didn't tell him about the conclusions I had reached after sailing north and watching the bears pull the salmon out of the river. I decided it would better to leave a lot of things for him to discover. We stood still near the river and marvelled at the mystery.

I told Ned I had just read a scientific paper by a Canadian geochemist saying that in this valley there had been more than a thousand tonnes of organic material to the acre. We paced out an acre on the ground, about sixty-five by sixty-five metres, and then tried to imagine what it was like before it had been logged.

'That's not a lot of land,' said the boy.

'No it is not,' I said. 'But it's more than enough for a family to live on. The acre was once defined as the amount of land one man, with an animal to help him, could plough in one day. In the old days families lived on acre strips that were one chain wide—that's twenty-two yards the exact length of a cricket pitch—and one furlong or a "furrow" long which was ten chains.'

We decided that when we had enough room to cast into the river we could cast about twenty-two yards, which was also about the width of the river. The chain seemed to be still used everywhere in the woods. Ned and I talked about this ancient unit and Ned said, 'We could call it a cast.'

The author of this article in the science journal didn't explain any further, he just stated the fact. I said I had checked this against published yields from farmers and they were not nearly so large and I wanted to know why. Rice, I discovered, only seemed to yield about three tonnes per acre (7.5 tonnes per hectare) and it was feeding probably half the population of the world. What was going on? The culture all over the planet for the last two thousand years at least had been concerned with conquering nature and making humans supreme, so why was it that we seemed to be getting less and less efficient?

Ned asked so many questions. He was drawing information out of his grandfather and filling his own head. 'You know what, Grandpa?' he said. 'I don't think we are very efficient animals. We waste too much.'

Ned's comment made me remember the Psalms. Didn't they say something about wisdom and strength coming out of the mouths of babes and sucklings?

'You know what, Ned?' I said. 'I think you have hit the nail right on the head.'

It had been difficult for me when I was living in the deep woods forty years earlier to answer many of these questions. Doing any kind of research into what was happening in other places involved writing lots of letters. In those days I didn't have a phone, personal computers were in the distant future and the library in Victoria was a day's journey away. Instead I had to fish and think, and both are best done alone, although I was now enjoying the company of an eight-year-old with an enquiring mind and he was helping me, just as I was helping him, to understand the wonders of the bush.

During the time I lived in Meade's cabin I didn't manage to find out much about the human history of the lake. The history of the place was not discussed. Enquiries were taboo. As the big logger had indicated the day he appeared in my doorway, writers were not welcome any more in this small rural community. It was therefore not easy to research anything, even though most of my work was in old-fashioned natural history, now called geology, geochemistry and biology. All my questions were treated with suspicion. Most of the locals considered enquirers to be some kind of loathsome pest that deserved to be eliminated as quickly as possible. Natural history was not well understood by most people round the lake, although there was the odd exception, like the old faller Swanson.

Nevertheless I was perhaps my own worst enemy because I did not know how to encourage people to volunteer information. I knew an elderly lady who I think may have been the wife of Henry March. I even had tea with her on one occasion, but I did not ask a single question—this was a mistake. I knew even then that perhaps the first duty of a writer is to pry, but in those days I didn't have the skill, I didn't even mention I was staying in Meade's old cabin. Now, I think that this lady would have enjoyed talking about the cabin's former occupants.

Negley Farson in *The Story of a Lake* called the March family the Treads and I wonder if he did this deliberately or just unconsciously made the connection between tread and march? He was drinking heavily at the time, I believe, and it is possible that he just didn't care. I wanted to know more about Farson, but I didn't like to ask.

On another occasion, I walked across the peninsula from my cabin to fish at Marble Bay and I was invited into the old place just overlooking the water. I didn't know then that it was where Doctor Stoker had lived, but an elderly lady who lived there in 1968 wanted me to help her move some heavy object. Now I think it was really because she needed some company or was curious about me. I had always liked the exterior of the old Indian-style bungalow, but inside it was an even more amazing place. It had big comfortable armchairs, lots of books and large counters in the centre of the room as well as at the sides, and under the long windows overlooking the lake. These benches were covered with all sorts of fascinating junk. The old lady shouted all the time as if I was deaf so I spoke loudly too. While I was there the telephone started to ring. I had never noticed a wire outside and there was no phone in sight. The ring seemed muffled and the old lady just ignored it. I spotted a vibrating tea-cosy at the far end of the counter and indicated that there must be a phone inside it that was ringing.

'Oh that damn thing,' she said. 'I can't hear it because I'm deaf.'

She went over to the phone, removed the tea-cosy,

lifted the receiver without putting it to her ear, slammed it back down again and replaced the cosy.

'They installed it a couple of weeks ago because people worry about me, but it's a damn nuisance.'

She picked up a metal ear trumpet from the counter. 'I've got this thing,' she said, 'but I find it is easier if people just shout.'

Much later I learned that Doctor Stoker's wife had used an ear trumpet. But this lady, I think, may have been Mrs Simpson. She didn't tell me her name when she invited me in and I was too shy to ask. Possibly she was the widow of the Englishman that Farson called Swinton, the self-appointed 'game warden' in his book. I learned later that the Simpsons moored their houseboat in Marble Bay to be away from the village and nearer to the Stokers. Perhaps later this lady had moved into the bungalow when the Stokers died. I still don't know enough of the history of the lake to be sure.

Socially I wasn't doing that well, but I was beginning to understand what was happening to the surrounding forest, the fabulous fishing, and the granite—the mother material—that lay beneath it all. My brain was soaking up everything like a sponge and I knew that all I had to do was take the time to squeeze it out, and I would have the answer.

The sojourn in Meade's cabin had been particularly

useful for I had grown up with the idea that salmon and trout were only to be caught by 'gentlemen'. Going fishing with guys like Arthur got this idea completely out of my head. In *Going Fishing* Negley Farson writes about this strange English view and describes the whole social order built upon it. It had little to do with money, the English said. It was birth and your connections or, in a word, *class*.

As a boy I was astonished to discover there were two kinds of people who pursued two kinds of fish: fish with an adipose fin were reserved for the upper class, and fish without that fin ordinary people were sometimes allowed to catch. Luckily, before I went to British Columbia I had lots of 'connections'. When I worked in Scotland I was fortunate enough to know people who 'owned' rivers. I thought that was ridiculous, no one could own a natural feature like a river, but as it was the custom throughout Europe I kept quiet so that I didn't lose the chance to fish. I remember one river I had permission to fish but only as far out as the middle because the other bank was owned by somebody else. I was told I had to be careful not to make too long a cast. Yet in Britain, even though the rivers were 'owned' by the rich, often ordinary people were allowed to fish for 'coarse' fish—that is to say, any fish that didn't have an adipose fin. This rule reserved trout and salmon for the rich. 'Game' fish are identified by the presence of this small fin on the back just in front of the tail. Useless for swimming, it is used for storing excess fat.

Nowadays, over most of the world, access to fresh water, and consequently fishing, is being restricted more and more each year. Canada is probably the only place left where nobody would question another person's right to fish. Everyone, even if they own land alongside a river, must have a licence to fish. On the back of that licence there is a paragraph explaining how to fish ethically, which has to be read and then signed. For senior, junior and disabled citizens there is no charge for a licence but others pay a small fee. Then anyone with a licence can fish. In places like Britain and Australia, people have first to buy a licence to fish and then get permission from a landowner to get to a river, which is often refused. Then, when it is legal to fish, we are often forced to pay another fee to fish in the owner's part of the river or in specially constructed lakes or ponds.

Because its water is not divided into classes according to quality, Canada is the most democratic place on Earth. South of the border, Americans, like Australians, have followed the English tradition of reserving the better rivers for the rich. Half a century ago, when I lived in Scotland, a permit for a 'beat' of a few hundred metres on one bank of a river allowing you to fish for a week cost hundreds of pounds. I imagine it would cost thousands now.

From time to time towards the end of my stay in Meade's cabin I fished many other rivers on Vancouver Island, including the river fished by Roderick Haig-Brown. The son of a wealthy English family he had learned to fish on the Piddle, an English chalk stream in Dorset where my godfather had been the vicar. He moved to the west coast of Canada as a young man and worked as a logger, and he successfully applied his angling skill to the much bigger fish that lived in the granite rivers that flowed off the great batholith. He wrote the wonderful *A River Never Sleeps* in 1944 and will be remembered as one of the greatest writers on fishing that has ever lived. He died in 1976. When I met him he was an august figure: the young English immigrant had become magistrate of Campbell River and chancellor of the new university in Victoria. But on this wild island loggers liked him too because he had once been one of them.

More than any other writer had done, Haig-Brown made it clear that the west coast of North America was an angler's heaven. He fished many remote places in the southern hemisphere where trout and salmon had been introduced but he always said the fishing in British Columbia, because of the nature and wildness of the land, was supreme. He would almost certainly have told lesser anglers that fishing in any water anywhere was wonderful, and that fishing had nothing to do with the size or number of fish caught. That the important thing was not just the joy of the hunt, but all the other things the angler discovers on the way. The fish was not the reward; it was just a symbol of really getting to understand the nature of the land. I don't know if he ever got a fish stuffed, but I rather think not. He knew better than I did. In those heady days in the late sixties it seems I caught a fish with every cast, but eventually I too came to understand that fishing was about something far more important than fish.

Ned said to me as we walked back towards the cabin, 'Why is it, Grandpa, that fishing is so much fun even though we are not actually catching fish?'

I told him it took some people a lifetime to work it out and asked him what he thought.

'I don't know, Grandpa, but I think the water and the wildness has something to do with it because it is definitely not as much fun just walking in a park.'

I resisted the temptation to tell him that that was because modern parks were really designed for ball games, and instead decided to give him some other facts to think about.

'I think you are right,' I said. 'When you were born your body was seventy-five per cent water and as you grow bigger that amount of water will gradually become less, but water will always attract us.'

'How much water is inside an old man like you, Grandpa?'

'I am not sure,' I said. 'But I am willing to bet it is still more than fifty per cent. Females for some reason have a little less than men, but I don't think any humans ever drop below forty-five per cent or they die.'

'That's probably why girls stay at home more and don't fish as much,' Ned replied.

Thinking about possible future charges of sexism, I tried to steer the conversation in another direction. 'I am not sure about that, Ned, but one thing I do know is that the girls always seem to catch bigger fish than we men do.' I told him how Georgina Ballantine caught the world's largest salmon in 1922 on the River Tay and also how another lady from Victoria caught the biggest fish in the Cowichan.

'That's not really fair, Grandpa,' said Ned.

'That's life,' I replied.

We were now almost back at the cabin and we could hear Matthew's axe. 'Dad's chopping wood. That's not really fair either.'

'Maybe he's enjoying it; I know I do. But I think he is just making himself useful and giving us a bit of time together so we can catch a fish. Fishing is a bit like cooking; too many cooks spoil the broth.'

13

Fishing Little Lakes

I prefer to fish flowing water but most freshwater anglers confine their fishing to the still water of ponds and lakes. Many anglers prefer to sit and contemplate the water and this is much easier for landowners to control. It is a very different kind of fishing. There is little exploring of new country, except when plumbing the bottom of the lake, and it is not nearly as energetic. The fisher remains in a comfortable spot and waits for the fish to come to him. I always want to see what is around the next bend in the river as well as find out what is in it.

Before the days of heavy regulation, most anglers preferred to fish rivers. In my view, it is only when a fisherman gets really desperate that he fishes lakes.

The problem with lakes is that anglers have to rely more on luck than skill. Experienced anglers don't like this because they like to predict where fish are lying and cast to that particular spot. In lakes that is not possible because fish behave quite differently. For any fish it is more efficient to lie still in a protected place in a river and capture any food that is swept past. Causing lots of jokes amongst non-fishers, anglers like to refer to a spot like this as 'a good lie'. These 'lies' do not exist in ponds and lakes because in still water fish must keep moving in order to make the less-oxygenated water pass through their gills.

As a boy in southern England I preferred to fish rivers, especially the clear streams that flowed out of the chalk. But as all of them were strictly preserved, I was forced to poach. With my long bamboo rod tied to the crossbar of my bicycle I searched the English countryside and fished every piece of water I came across. I even fished a flooded bomb-crater on the edge of the local airfield during the Battle of Britain. I waded in bare feet right under Spitfires that were taking off. Amazingly, I caught my first pike there, even though this particular hole in the ground had only been there a couple of months. I cut my foot rather badly on some debris under the water so I limped back to my bicycle and painfully made my way home. I left my little jack-pike in the new pool to grow bigger, although what there was for it to feed on I had no idea.

A kilometre or two further up the road was the Hainault Lake and I fished that regularly for rudd and perch. It was a popular spot and had been a fishery since Norman times. The rudd often fed in shoals near the surface and were a delight to watch and catch. They are beautifully coloured fish with rich red sides as the name suggests. The perch were less common but perhaps that was because they knew I liked to eat them. There were also quite large pike in the lake, which ate the other fish and occasionally pulled under a duck or a coot, but I never caught one of those. If I had hooked an adult pike I wouldn't have been able to land it with my rod as I didn't have a reel. Older and more experienced anglers told me that pike spawn were transferred to places like my bomb crater on the feet of ducks, and that was how I was able to catch a baby jack in such an unlikely place.

Once, before the war, I fished Hainault Lake with a somewhat heartless friend. As his float gently wobbled he struck rather clumsily and his hook pulled out a fish's eye. Having lost his last maggot on the strike, and being quite unmoved by this event, he then used the eye as bait. A few moments later he caught a one-eyed perch that had eaten its own eye.

There are countless lakes in Canada, more than in any

other country, and most of them are on the great Canadian Shield, the world's largest area of exposed glaciated pre-Cambrian rock. It is part of the planet's original crust and the retreat of the ice sheet at the end of the Pleistocene left it covered with more than a million lakes. I canoed across about half of it once, an expedition that took a couple of months. I had to abandon my voyage and fly out because winter was coming.

The journey filled me with admiration for the pioneers and the handful of native people I met on the trip. The fishing was amazing. Whatever fly or lure was attached to my line was grabbed almost immediately by a fish. More often than not it was a pike, but walleye and brook trout were also common.

The Nehalliston Plateau in central British Columbia is another wonderful place for lakes, with perhaps ten thousand of them left by the melting ice. These lakes are unique because they contain only trout. Many would argue that this plateau has the best trout fishing anywhere on the planet. Lakes are not common in the far west of the province because there the land is drained by straight, fast rivers.

The time had come for Ned and me to fish a lake. We had no canoe so the lake we chose to fish was the small three-acre pond not far from the cabin I had spotted walking back from the canyon the day before Ned arrived. It was surrounded with rushes and there were not many gaps where an angler could comfortably fish. The tiny side feeder of the main river had been dammed, probably about eighty years ago when this lower part of the valley was being logged and the water used for fighting fires.

There was one of those cast-metal signs with raised letters that Canadians do so well on the access path. It stated the name of the lake and it said fishing there was reserved for handicapped anglers, senior citizens and juveniles. So Ned and I were permitted to fish. It was much easier to fish from the dam itself but Ned and I chose to wander through the rushes and find our own quiet places. In the still water of these ponds it is easier to see when fish rise to the fly. Ned had noticed some rises further up the lake and had picked a place; but the fish only rose occasionally and were out of reach. I made a few casts from another spot, putting the fly out quite a long way but didn't have any success. Actually I didn't want to catch a fish because I wanted Ned to succeed before I did, so I spent more time looking at the water and fiddling with my tackle.

After we had been on the water about half an hour a pick-up truck arrived and a man in his forties got out and started casting from the dam. He obviously wasn't handicapped, a senior or a juvenile but it wasn't my job to point that out. He seemed quite a pleasant person. He said his name was Lorne and told me he often stopped at this lake on his way home from work. He showed me his gear: a spinning rod with a fixed-spool reel filled with thin nylon. He said he usually made a dozen or so casts from the dam and often caught a fish. Mostly he caught brook trout. The pond had been stocked with this eastern American variety of trout because they were easier to catch. 'It's almost infallible,' he said. 'You cast out as far as possible; use one of these torpedo-shaped plastic casting aids half-filled with water so it acts like a weight and put a Doc Spratley on the end. If you don't get one on in less than a couple of dozen casts,' he added, 'they are not biting and you go on home.'

I told him I should have known the Doc Spratley was a good fly for I remembered a friend having a lot of success with it in this valley forty years ago. I then thanked him for reminding me of its existence and said it was good to see the fly was still popular in this neck of the woods.

I didn't tell him that once Big Arthur took to fly fishing the Doc Spratley was his favourite fly, and I certainly didn't say that any other fly would probably have worked just as well when whacked out into the middle of the pond. Instead, I just smiled. He spent less than ten minutes fishing, then climbed back into the truck and left. 'Try again tomorrow,' he shouted. 'And get yourself a couple of Doc Spratleys.'

Doctor Spratley was a dentist from Washington State who was one of the first Americans to fish in British Columbia. The fly named after him lived on around Cowichan Lake. The original pattern was tied on a number six hook, usually a sproat. It had a Guinea fowl tail and hackle and the head was a few turns of peacock herl. Sometimes it had a small wing of brown pheasant feather but the most important thing was the black wool torpedo-shaped body wrapped with silver tinsel. In fact if you left out the unnecessary wing it was almost identical to my fly, a copy of the stone fly tied by the Abbess of Saint Albans six hundred years ago. We certainly do weave a tangled web when we try to deceive something as simple as a fish.

'What was that man talking about, Grandpa?' asked Ned.

'He was just teaching your poor old grandfather to suck eggs, but I didn't hold it against him because he was kind and friendly.'

'Do you suck eggs, Grandpa?'

'No,' I said. 'I still have a few teeth left, so I usually boil them first.'

Ned asked me about the strange expressions we use in the English language.

'It's just a way we say things sometimes, it's called a

metaphor, I think. A figure of speech.'

'Why do you call a thing a metaphor if it's a figure of speech?'

'You've got me there,' I said. 'You will have to ask someone who knows more about the English language than I do.'

'Are you still learning, Grandpa?'

'We all are. No one can know everything, but it's important to try.'

Ned and I continued fishing the edges of the lake for about another two hours and then gave up. I was not nearly as persistent as my grandson, and I continually allowed my mind to drift away from the job in hand.

'What did you think of the lake?' I asked Ned as we left.

'I thought it was a very good piece of water,' he said, and I knew he would be a first-rate fisherman given a little more time.

We packed up our gear and got in the car to drive back to the cabin. Just as we drew away from the lake, as often happens, the fish started to rise.

'That's typical,' I said. 'We've put all our gear away and now they start to rise.'

'Maybe they know we are going,' said Ned.

'I think you're right,' said his frustrated grandfather. The amazing thing was the kid was more philosophical about it than the man.

As we drove away from the lake I realised that I didn't know its name. It must have been at the top of the metal plate but I hadn't taken it in. Although I know how to get to a hell of a lot of places that are interesting to anglers, I generally don't notice the names, and when I do find a place that I love I often refer to it by a special name that I make up. Two that spring to mind are Mystery Creek and the Lost River—they are both great places for fish but neither could support large numbers of anglers so it is probably clever not to identify them. I no longer remember the official names of these two rivers. Visiting them on this trip wasn't possible, we couldn't have stayed near either of them for they were both isolated and there was no accommodation.

Years ago I read Clive Gammon's angling classic *I Know a Good Place* and I enjoyed it a lot. Gammon never actually identified any of these spots but cleverly made his readers fellow conspirators. I have always been rather secretive about the ones I know.

Of course with Ned it was different, and for a moment I thought it would have been better if I had taken him to a fabulous river like the Lost where I often used to get a fish with my very first cast. It probably wouldn't be like that now because of commercial fishing near the mouth, but it was fished far less heavily than the Cowichan and was rarely visited by anglers. Thinking about it, however, I understood I had done the right thing trying to show Ned how to fish on this much more popular river. If anything is made too easy it is always less satisfying. I would leave the Lost River for him to discover.

I started thinking about worms. Angling with a worm, especially when the water is other than very clear, is probably the simplest way to catch a fish. Quite why that is, is hard to say, because earthworms are not the natural food of fish. I have opened the stomachs of hundreds of fish to check what they have been feeding on and have never found a worm inside. Flies by the hundred yes, but never a worm, although I have occasionally found lots of snails complete with shells inside a trout. Oddly, I have never used, or known another fisherman to use, a snail as bait.

The next time, we decided, it would have to be a worm. We decided to commission Ned's dad to find some of this more suitable bait. Thinking back, though, we had plenty of bacon at the cabin and it might have been worth trying a small worm-shaped portion of that. It probably would have worked very well. Maybe I had fished too long with flies.

Fish may not be that familiar with worms although worms obviously do get washed into rivers especially when the banks are swept away in times of flood. Fish have an excellent sense of smell, even better than that of a bloodhound or a bear. Scientists tell us that a bear's sense of smell is forty times more sensitive than that of a bloodhound because it can smell things from several kilometres away, but this pales into insignificance when compared with various members of the salmon family which can smell their way back to the stream of their birth from far out at sea.

Despite their magnificent smelling ability members of the trout and salmon family do not use smell to find food. They hunt by sight, which is why we fish with artificial flies resembling the insects they fed on in their natal streams.

I remember being fascinated by artificial flies many years ago on a mountain stream in Wales when an experienced angler opened his beautiful nine-by-six centimetre aluminium fly box handmade by Richard Wheatley in England. This young man, a couple of years older than I was, carefully popped open a spring loaded see-through lid on one of the six compartments and drew out one of his collection of a dozen or so flies. I think it was a Coch-y-Bondhu, an imitation of a small beetle widely used in Wales. The water was fast and clear, and the small feisty Welsh trout were much more interested in his flies than they were in my bedraggled worm. He gave me one of his precious flies and I have been a fly fisherman ever since. For years I stuck my flies in my hat but just recently I have become more respectable and bought one of these expensive handmade aluminium boxes. It fits very nicely in the top pocket of my jacket or shirt.

Anglers don't fish just to catch fish; if we did, we would net them. We hunt fish, which are very smart, in order to outwit them, and we are less successful than we like to think. Many great anglers have said fishing is a ridiculous passion because fish cost far more to catch than they would to buy in a market, but we continue the pursuit because it enables us to think. The mystery of water fascinates us.

Although I occasionally enjoy eating trout and salmon, I am not that fond of fish. The best meat I ever ate was from a wild sheep shot in the Arctic. It was infinitely superior to lamb from the butcher. But I only ate wild sheep once. Having grown up in the Great Depression, I eat only to live and have never wanted to be a person who did the reverse. I try to live simply and I believe the life of a gourmet would be boring. Perhaps this is why I usually just admire fish and then release them, but I do believe that if a person loves wild country like I do, he or she should always be capable of 'living off the land'. It is a skill our ancestors had, and I do not want it to disappear.

14

The Pilgrims' Final Day

There were lots of things I wanted to tell my grandson, but I knew I had to let him discover them for himself in a magical way. Although we have imagined ourselves as created in the image of God and conceitedly named ourselves *Homo sapiens*, knowledgeable man, it has never been helpful to think of our species as being special and particularly different from other life forms. We are slightly different and that is all.

The best way to pass on information to our offspring is to sniff around a bit and set an example, the way other creatures do it. That's what I had been doing with Ned for the last few days; we called it fishing but it was really much more. And it wasn't all one way—I learned a lot from him.

Much of my life, like Walt Whitman, I have thought I could live with animals because they are placid and self-contained, but I am not an animal lover in the usual sense. I never pat passing dogs, I am not keen on cats and though I once enjoyed riding horses I don't really like the way they smell. When I kept chickens I thought they were rather silly, but I was grateful for their eggs. I prefer wild animals like cougars and bears because they have been less affected by man. I think of myself as just another animal, and I thank my lucky stars I was born a man rather than a mouse.

The greatest difference seems to be that humans think more than other animals and can understand more complicated things. I am always thankful for the existence of science, but I find that advances in technology irritate me, especially when they are called advances in science. Contrary to common belief, technology is not derived from science, it is older and has been around for thousands of years. Science is only two and a half thousand years old. The people who practised it a few years ago when we were paying more attention to the latest research are now being overlooked. Recently, we have become preoccupied with wealth, and have become enamoured with a pseudo-science called economics that seems to be only concerned with the 'growth' of a convenient but impractical thing called money.

Most of us, including a growing number of university professors, spend a lot of our time perpetuating myths. The biggest myth is that we live in a new scientific age; if that were true we would be more careful about the things we do.

Technology in the twenty-first century reigns supreme and it is our love of gizmos and gadgets that is rapidly destroying the planet. We use this extra energy every day, forgetting that every time we do this we contribute to climate change. Science taught us this long ago, yet most of us carry on ignoring, or blissfully unaware of, the cumulative effect of our actions. Every time one types in a search term on a personal computer for Google to find, an estimated seven grams of carbon dioxide is released into the atmosphere. I don't know how many Google searches there are per day around the planet, but it is clear the total energy used to transport information, a lot of which is incorrect, is now beginning to rival that used to transport people and goods, which is also increasing. To cap it all there is now lots of advertising transmitted at the same time adding to the load. When I checked just now I discovered there are half a dozen different search engines and together they make about 213 million searches a day. Multiply that by seven grams. We are producing too much greenhouse gas and have to slow down.

Thales of Miletus was the first real scientist although he would not have recognised the term. He argued he was a philosopher who tried to understand the world not in myths but in terms that were subject to verification. We would do well to follow the wisdom of Thales today.

Some of this was in my mind as I walked along the river with Ned. It is probably why I bought him the world's most primitive tool, an old-fashioned knife. In an attempt to teach him something about science we made a spark with the knife and set fire to a handful of steel wool. I did this because it is generally believed that iron will not burn.

Thales established mathematics as a science, but more importantly he was the first man to think objectively about nature. As I walked along the river with Ned I attempted to emulate this Greek. Thales objected to the common way of explaining the world through myths. He believed the world was essentially made of water—quite amazing really for in 600 BC there was no knowledge about the size or even the shape of our planet. He argued that water was the most important thing because it was the only substance that could be seen in three forms—solid, liquid and gas—and he wrote eloquently about the clouds in the sky as being part of a much greater sea. All those years ago Thales was right. Ned and I talked about these ideas quite a lot.

Now we have discovered that the compound called water is made of the two elements hydrogen and oxygen, and we accept that there is a series of ninety-two elements starting with hydrogen and ending with uranium found naturally on our Earth. But we make new ones heavier than uranium, which last a few seconds and then disintegrate, just to show how clever we are.

In talking to Ned I often thought about what the old philosopher would say if asked the same penetrating questions that came from my young grandson. I am not saying I gave answers as good as Thales would have given, but I always thought about Ned's questions seriously and tried to answer with the truth. That is after all what science is about—the ultimate search for truth.

Truth is evasive and is only found by examining fiction just as carefully as the supposed facts. Kris Kristofferson wrote a song about this describing a pilgrim as a walking contradiction, partly truth and partly fiction. The ancient Greeks were like that too and, as my grandson and I walked along the river, so were we.

On our last day at the cabin we carefully cleaned everything up, split some kindling for the next visitors and went again into the town. The river was down a bit in one area where it exited from the lake and near the new footbridge it was now possible to swim. Although the water was still icy cold, Ned decided to take a dip. His father sat on the bank as a lifeguard and I went back across the footbridge to revisit the tackle shop. I wanted to tell Gordy that I knew his grandmother.

I realised that I was now part of history and that meeting interesting people like the tackle dealer had been a highlight of my trip. But when I went inside the store this time and told him I once had tea with old Mrs March he told me he had nothing to do with that family and that he was not related to them. I wasn't sure I believed this and it made me think of the Cowichan people as others like Negley Farson had done before me. Gordy was a wonderful guy and if he really was one of the original March family he probably wanted to be free of the legends of the past. The lake had always been a place where everyone had to shape their own lives because they all knew that here everyone had to be an individual. I didn't argue with Gordy even though I was sure I had known his grandmother. I was reminded that the Cowichan was different—it really was.

The place had always been like the song, a walking contradiction, partly truth and partly fiction. I was beginning to think I would get no further in my search to find out the answer to that conundrum, when I spotted a small memorial park close to the bridge.

It was a monument to the history of the place, so I decided to have a look. There were various plaques and a brick footpath embroidered with names. I read them all: young loggers killed on the job, and people who had paid for a brick with their name on it so at least that would live on. I recognised a few names, mainly ordinary folk, but the pioneers and the people I knew, perhaps the more exceptional people, appeared to be missing. There was no mention of the Stokers, or of Meade, and there was certainly nothing about Negley Farson and the original settlers from Europe he wrote about with such thinly disguised names. I wanted to know more about the Englishman Henry March and the scientifically inclined Englishman Simpson. There didn't seem to be any mention of them or indeed anyone from that time. It was almost as if the generation that erected this memorial had been so disturbed by being written about that they had decided to end all their previous history and start all over again.

Now, because of my writing, perhaps fact and fiction will become even more entwined, or maybe this book will help the truth come out. Whatever happens, I wish all the people of Lake Cowichan well.

On the way back we decided to go and look at Meade's cabin. I imagined we would now be able to drive to Marble Bay and look at Doctor Stoker's place and then walk over the col to the cabin. I thought we might also climb Bald Mountain. But when we got to Marble Bay we found it had changed. That beautiful fishing spot, the best place on the lake, the only breeding place for the alkali-loving mayflies with its small area of limestone was now a marina full of boats leaking oil. The rainbow slick had obviously put paid to the breeding of most of these delicate and beautiful flies. Obviously the whole food-chain had been affected.

The Stokers' log bungalow seemed to have disappeared. I think it must have been torn down. On the col between there and the North Arm was a new holiday town—a suburb with those ghastly names that developers are so fond of and which attempt to perpetuate natural features that their bulldozers have destroyed, like Coppice View Crescent, Vista Avenue and so on. Most of the houses had not yet been sold although a few were occupied, with their driveways full of giant four-wheel drive vehicles and huge plastic boats. The owners, I suppose, were older people and had been lured to the lake by the prospect of fish.

Eventually I found Meade's Creek and we followed it to the beach at the end of the North Arm. This too was part of a suburbia of mega-houses with their own private harbours and wharves. The beach had been cleared completely of driftwood and it had a strange manicured look as all the trees overhanging the water had gone. Meade's cabin had been enlarged and so modified and messed about with it was hard to recognise; I only knew it because I remembered its exact position. Meade's old orchard was still there but this now seemed like a communal asset and had neatly mown lawns like a park. I thought of my sojourn there and of Farson again. What would he think if he could see this place today? Even more, what would Meade have to say? I imagine if the three of us could have discussed it we would agree it had been ruined. Worst of all, when I looked at the map of the whole development I noticed Bald Mountain was now marked as private property, and when I looked down-lake I saw most of the trees had gone.

I remember once saying that going back to a place was always a disappointment, but in some odd way I felt vindicated. In recent years I had come to the conclusion that my column forty years earlier had sometimes gone a bit far, but now that I was back in the Cowichan I realise it had not gone far enough.

Yet there were a few spring salmon in the town pool proving that whatever we do nature still has something in reserve. It was rather like the aftermath of a brawl in a bar during the gold rush: the eighty-eight keys on the piano might have been pretty well all smashed but it was still possible, if you used your initiative, to pound out a bit of a tune. The old days were wonderful, but where we are at this moment is still pretty good. I was sad that I had missed my old fishing partner Big Arthur because it would have been interesting to hear his views on this.

Time was now running short and Ned still hadn't caught a fish, but he was proving to be an excellent fisherman because he kept trying.

On the way home on that last day we visited one last lake. It was slightly larger than the one near the cabin. We found a fairly shallow bay with quite a lot of weeds and a rocky shore and decided to fish there. It was our last attempt and the time had come to try a worm suspended beneath a float.

We had only about half an hour left and while I was still fiddling with my tackle Ned caught his first fish. He used a float big enough to scare a pike because it helped him cast with the tiny rod, but nevertheless he got a fish on. He played it well and started to bring it in. It was a young trout, and Ned was bubbling with excitement.

'I've got one Grandpa,' he shouted.

He decided it was too small for us to eat, so he carefully let it go. And I was very proud of him.

It was a perfect end to our trip. Perhaps Ned will never see fish like I used to see in the beautiful valley, but it was important to discover that some fish are still there.

My grandson and I had been exploring one of the outer layers of a ball of iron hurtling relentlessly through space. Although the locals called this piece of water the Cowichan and our species called this globe the Earth, the most obvious layer is water. The next most obvious are granite and air, and we belong to an even less obvious but ubiquitous layer of life. We had been gathering knowledge as we walked along the river; we called it fishing but it was more than that. We were trying to reconnect with our planet.

When I was small the human culture presented to me by parents, parsons and pedants tried to make me feel unique, but I always felt happier recognising I was part of a larger whole. That is why I climbed mountains, wandered through wilderness areas, sailed lonely seas and fished remote rivers. Mostly I did it alone because if you are alone you are entirely your own man. I was searching for my identity for I was not happy having it defined by others.

Our trip was now over, and I had to return to Australia. I reminded myself that all good things have to come to an end. It had been a success because Ned had landed a fish, but the really important thing was that we had experienced the river flowing through the trees and it still had mysterious and wonderful possibilities. We had gone out into the great forest and learned something new. We had asked questions and thought about all the different answers. We had learned to fish and think together, and together we had understood the goal wasn't the fish at all. The log cabin on the river was excellent, better than staying at Meade's old place today, and I decided all grandfathers should spend more time with their grandchildren living in the bush.

I had done what Aksakov said and ventured into native waters in the cool shade of the forest and gone back to the years of my youth. And I had taken my grandson with me into this world of serenity and freedom.

Acknowledgments

Many thanks to the people of Lake Cowichan, the Land Conservancy in Victoria and David and Disa Jaye, to John Elwin, Dorothy Johnston and Bruce Sims, whose comments on early drafts were so encouraging, to my agent Mary Cunnane and to my editors Jane Pearson and Michael Heyward at Text.